BELFAST:
FROM LOYALTY TO REBELLION

City Cultures

Series Editor: Tony Lane

As attention shifts away from Europe's old nation states and towards its cities and regions, this innovative new series will explore the social and cultural character of Europe's great cities. A well informed grasp of the astonishing variety of urban cultures is vital for an understanding of the emerging new Europe. Before we can look forward to the transformation of our nation states we need a better understanding than is currently available of the undiminished potency of ideas of nation and national identity. A challenging approach to this problem can be found in an unravelling of the forces that have created the richly varied cultural characters of Europe's cities, cities which inspire intense loyalties among their peoples.

Already published:

Seán Damer, *Glasgow: Going for a Song*
Tony Lane, *Liverpool: Gateway of Empire*

Belfast: From Loyalty to Rebellion

Maurice Goldring

LAWRENCE & WISHART
LONDON

Lawrence and Wishart Limited
144a Old South Lambeth Road
London SW8 1XX

First published 1991
Copyright © Maurice Goldring, 1991

Photoset in North Wales by
Derek Doyle and Associates, Mold, Clwyd
Printed and bound in Great Britain by
Billing and Sons, Worcester

To M.S., who did not cook, did not look after my house, did not type my manuscript, did not correct the proofs and was not particularly patient with my fits of ill humour, because she had her own work to do.

Contents

Acknowledgements

Many friends, colleagues and institutions have made possible the publication of this book. Professor Ronald Buchanan and the Institute of Irish Studies of Queen's University, Belfast, provided a stimulating environment for my research and never tired of my unceasing demands. A number of people read and made comments on the first and subsequent drafts of this book: Professor David Harkness and Hilary Harkness, Professor John Darby and Mary Darby were generous with their help, comments and hospitality; Paul Bew, Tony Lane and Martine Spensky read the manuscript and offered valuable suggestions. The British Council, the Centre for Irish Studies (part of the Centre Nationale de Recherche Scientifique) run by Jacqueline Genet and the late Patrick Rafroidi, and the research seminar on the History of Labour in English-Speaking Countries, University of Paris VIII (Saint Denis) all contributed towards the cost of frequent trips to Belfast. Brian Follis and his staff at the Public Record Office of Northern Ireland, Belfast's Linen Hall Library, the keepers of archives of the Catholic Church, the Presbyterian Church, the Church of Ireland, the Northern Ireland Committee of the Irish Congress of Trade Unions, various political leaders and activists, and the Official Unionist Party (which gave me permission to use the archives of the Ulster Unionist Labour Association) were all of immense assistance. And last but not least, Stephen Hayward, who corrected, edited and commented on the manuscript, and became a friend in the process.

Introduction

On and off, I have been a fan of Belfast for the last twenty years. I have a vivid memory of my first visit in July 1970 to see the Orange Order parade on the Lisburn Road. The crowd looked hostile, but I was proud to be there. After all, I could tell my students back in Paris that I had been surrounded by the sullen throng and seen the Orangemen marching, could describe the elaborate banners and sashes and the sound of the Lambeg drums. They would look admiringly at their brave professor who had been right in the thick of things. 'Weren't you afraid, sir?' they would ask. I have never been afraid in Belfast. The city loves its visitors: its problem is self-hatred.

Twenty years ago the streets at night were empty, the pubs deserted and the restaurants closed. I remember eating with a friend in a restaurant that could seat 200 people; there were just two of us dining there and the waiters were queuing up to serve us. The city was getting ready for twenty years of demonstrations, killings, hunger strikes, conferences, strikes, unemployment and the rest of the litany. During those years children were born and grew up in South, East and West Belfast, went to school, played in the streets and went to church or to Mass. People were killed and others were arrested, tried and imprisoned. Countless books and articles were written. Twenty years later the streets and pubs are full and you have to queue to get into the best restaurants. 'Belfast is buzzing,' the advertising agencies would have us believe, and I'm glad to say that for once they are right. The commercial centre is thriving and the golden mile is spreading. At the same time, however, students are leaving the city once they graduate – 'I can't stand it any more,' they say - and find jobs in London, New York and Sydney, where they will assimilate easily. Only in Belfast will they be considered as strangers by their fellow citizens. They will sing the same songs if they meet in a bar abroad, but will tear each others' guts out if they meet back 'home' in Belfast.

You will get very different initial impressions of Belfast depending on how you arrive in the city. Suppose you come for an academic seminar. You take the shuttle flight from London's Gatwick airport; on board you have a hot meal, maybe half a bottle of wine, with a smiling businessman sitting next to you.

Sometimes the local businessmen grumble, complaining about the public face of their city. It seems, from what they say, that Belfast has been destroyed by the media rather than by its home-grown bombs. This is the official line. The Northern Ireland Tourist Board tries very hard to restore the province's tattered image: peaceful landscapes and good restaurants, a disciplined and well trained workforce are all ruined by the journalists' insistence on covering bombs, barricades and terrorism. Most Northerners, apparently, are well behaved, and were it not for cameras glued to hooded hoodlums the world would not be aware that Belfast is a dangerous city. It is all the journalists' fault. Then a friendly face welcomes you at Aldergrove, a good provincial airport, full of banks, boutiques and all the other facilities one finds at airports nowadays. You are driven past the shipyards to stay in a comfortable home in South Belfast, or maybe taken to the Europa or Wellington Park Hotel where you have a Bushmills on expenses and settle into your room. Who in those circumstances would be afraid of Big Bad Belfast?

But if you happen to be coming from the North of England and arrive in Belfast by plane from Liverpool you arrive at Belfast Harbour Airport, which is nothing like Aldergrove. It looks more like a ramshackle collection of wartime huts than a modern airport. There is no bus. Especially on a Sunday, the security guard tells me. The two or three waiting taxis were stormed a long time ago. The other passengers knew – they had friends or relatives waiting for them with cars. I am stranded in the wilderness, miles from the city centre. It does not rain, of course, it pours. The security officer invites me into his hut to take shelter from the rain and tells me that a taxi will be along soon. Whenever a car appears from out of the downpour he leaves his hut, waves the driver to move on or stops the car, heaves up the bonnet and looks into the guts of the vehicle with his torch. Still no sign of a taxi.

Luckily another passenger is stranded with me, a young woman with a round, intelligent face. I ask her what on earth she is doing here. She is training as a nurse in Liverpool, she tells me, and has come to Belfast to spend a week at the Royal Victoria Hospital because it is the only place in Western Europe where one can study casualties inflicted by bombs and bullets. The RVH has become internationally renowned for its emergency centre: doctors and nurses flock in from around the world to learn the new techniques of repair for bodies that have been wounded and maimed by rubber bullets, flying glass and tear gas. Every cloud has its silver lining. I am an academic, she is a nurse. She waits for a taxi, I start dreaming. We are cold and huddled in the security officer's hut, time passes and a car full of gunmen arrives. The security officer is killed but I somehow save her life. We meet for tea at the Forum Hotel, her eyes glisten as I look into them, violins start to play 'When Irish Eyes Are Smiling'.

Outside the hut and my imagination the rain continues to pour down. There is still no taxi to be seen. Are the three of us going to spend the night standing in the hut? The security officer renews his call for a taxi for us with his walkie-talkie. At last a cab pulls up, driven by a woman who will take us both into town. First she takes the nurse to the RVH, an enormous place, a city within a city. The nurse says goodbye – I will never see her again. The violins stop playing and the driver starts talking. Apparently she had taken her son to the hospital the night before; he had been attacked by three men, severely beaten up and now has a broken arm and is badly bruised. 'What happened?' I ask dutifully. The driver has no doubt that it was all the doing of her son's wife, ex-wife that is, and her friends. She divorced him three years ago, but the legal procedure is bitter and dragging slowly through the courts. The wife was the wrong type and it was bound to end in tears – my driver had told her son as much but he wouldn't listen. Some so-called friends had invited her son to a drinking club, UVF it was; when they came out at the end of the evening he was attacked. It was a put up job, organised by his wife, of this the driver was certain. That's when I realised that Belfast is a city where family feuds can be disguised as tribal revenge and where tribal feuds can masquerade as family life. Or both.

The primary purpose of this book is quite straight-forward – to show that Belfast exists, that it has a past, a present and a future. It is there to stay. If Belfast has no future, as many pundits suggest, then I know many a European or North American city which doesn't have one either. It is a big sprawling city in the northern part of Ireland where half a million people try to live. The status of that city is a moot point, but it is there, on the map and in real life. I stress this simple and obvious point because so many books with Ireland in their titles contain not a single reference to Belfast. The index jumps quickly from Barry to Birmingham, from Banbridge to Blackrock, and Belfast is missing. Funnily enough, the more republican the point of view, the more militantly committed the writer is to the reunification of the whole island, the more Belfast somehow disappears. In a recent study of the Poor Law in Ireland in the nineteenth century 'Ireland' is taken to mean the 26 counties of the present-day Republic.[1] The book is a serious work of historical scholarship, well researched and often illuminating, but fatally flawed by this extraordinary lapse. If you were to go by a recent book on Irish women's migration to Britain you might think that there is no such thing as Protestant women who move from Belfast to the mainland.[2] In the circumstances it then becomes very easy to reunify the island: you simply draw a line round a blank space a bit further north. By erasing the capital of the North from the map and turning the majority of its inhabitants into non-persons, such writers actually make reunification more difficult. Ignoring the majority of the population in a city is bad enough, erasing it altogether is even worse, and it is hardly surprising that this attitude (whether expressed in political speeches, newspaper articles or books) serves to increase loyalists' determination to stay where they are behind their current frontier.

Well, Belfast happens to be in Ireland, the United Kingdom and Europe. It is part and parcel of our common history, our 'common European home'. In Europe cities, communities and nations were first built and developed because they were held together by an external threat. Each of us is part of a common history of defence against imaginary threats or real enemies. The difference is that in Belfast the perceived threat comes from within the community.

I would like to have written a book that would bring peace to a wounded city, but alas I am not a magician. All I can say, to those who will listen, is that if you live in Europe then you live in Belfast as well. Belfast needs a lot of external looks at its own internal feuds. French and Parisian, I am also proud to call myself a Belfastman.

Notes

1   Helen Burke, *The People and the Poor Law in Nineteenth Century Ireland*, Littlehampton 1987.
2   Mary Lennon, Marie McAdam and Joanne O'Brien, *Across the Water: Irish Women's Lives in Britain*, London 1988.

1 It Happened

Beginnings

Belfast is a young city and it is both easy and tempting to sift through its past when looking for the causes of the present troubles. Easy but misleading, because its early history is not so very different from that of many other European cities.

The city's name is Gaelic in origin and means the mouth of the sandbank. Belfast started life as a small town, later to become a centre of commerce and industry with its docks and shipyards built on reclaimed mud. Cave Hill, the landmark that can be seen today from most parts of the city, a favourite place for walking and relaxing and in the eighteenth century a meeting place for rebels, has always overlooked the site. The other major physical feature when the town was established was the 'marshy solitude' at the mouth of the River Lagan.

The town was founded in 1603, and made a borough in 1613, by Sir Arthur Chichester who was later raised to the peerage as Baron Chichester of Belfast. The town was governed by 'a sovereign' and twelve free burgesses. This sovereign was the all-powerful ruler and the town was a family or 'pocket' borough. The first citizens were mostly English settlers, often retired soldiers, followed by growing numbers of Scottish Presbyterians. Belfast was then primarily a centre of trade for this settler community. By 1650 the population was about 1,000. Freemen did not have the right to vote but they were privileged citizens, exempt from the customs and tolls paid by 'strangers' bringing goods into the city. The different craftsmen living in the town – bakers, tailors, barbers and others – were protected from outsiders in the same way. The pattern was not very different from that of any budding city except, with the advantage of hindsight, that later developments give a sinister tone to this protection against 'strangers'. For who were these strangers but the natives, strangers in their own land? But then which town or city did not protect its privileged citizens against outsiders in those days?

In the seventeenth century Irish sea trade began to develop. As one historian has noted, European trade was expanding into the Atlantic so 'Ireland was no longer on the edge of the world but near the centre of the stage.'[1] Liverpool and Glasgow were beginning to compete for trade with the American colonies, and Belfast also became involved in the colonial trade. Gallagher's tobacco empire was just around the corner. Overseas trade led to the development of a small shipbuilding industry, but on the whole trade remained local and agricultural in character.

In 1690 William of Orange landed at Carrickfergus where he was enthusiastically welcomed by members of the Church of Ireland from Belfast. James II had revoked Belfast's old charter and replaced the corporation formed exclusively of Anglican Protestants loyal to the Church of Ireland by a new one composed of an equal number of Anglicans and Catholics, but excluding Presbyterians. The first attempt at power-sharing, one might say. After William's victory at the Boyne the former corporation, composed entirely of Anglicans, was restored. The Church of Ireland reigned supreme, and this supremacy was resented as bitterly by Presbyterians as it was by Catholics. It should be remembered that the Penal Laws excluded all non-Anglicans from political power, not just Catholics. The only Irish university, Trinity College, Dublin, was closed to Presbyterians, who, unlike Catholics, at least had the right to attend Scottish universities. In 1627, by order of the corporation, every burgess and free commoner had to attend Sunday worship with the sovereign. In 1685 the rules became even stricter and small fines were imposed on inhabitants of the borough for non-attendance at public worship. The penalty was twopence for a householder, a penny for a woman, a halfpenny for a servant and a farthing for a child.[2]

Ireland, it is sometimes forgotten because of the present partition, was then one administrative unit, and its capital was Dublin. The Irish parliament sat in Dublin, and the capital was, of course, the centre of the Anglo-Irish Ascendancy's political power. Belfast was at the far end of the corridor of power; remote from the capital, it was of little account in the great scheme of things as perceived by the Ascendancy. Before the nineteenth-century reforms political life in Belfast amounted to next to nothing, with the corporation a self-selecting body under the total control of the Donegall family, the owners of the land on which the city was built. The inhabitants of the town, Protestant and Catholic alike, had almost no way of making their voice heard. Belfast elected two members to the Dublin parliament; the only voters were the sovereign and the twelve burgesses who formed the corporation, but the reality was even less representative – the Donegalls nominated the two MPs. The Act of Union of 1801 did away with the Dublin parliament, but the MPs who were thenceforth sent to Westminster were also nominated by very few people. It was not until 1840, with the Municipal Corporation Act, that the old ruling body was swept away and replaced by a corporation of 40 members elected by the £10 householders.

With this reform modern politics were born. The new Act enabled O'Connell to become Lord Mayor of Dublin and also introduced mass politics to Belfast. What remains from the period before 1840 is the importance of non-municipal bodies. People who wanted power and influence sought to join bodies like the Harbour

Commission or the Board of Guardians rather than the council. Even today the city of Belfast is not, as such, an important political forum. Until 1972 there was the six-county parliament at Stormont and the wider arena of the province at large, but not much by way of Belfast politics. This dates back to the times when the capital was far away and a tradition of self-help developed; the fact that the town was dominated by Presbyterianism no doubt encouraged this process, giving Belfast a marked proclivity for committee work. Protestant businessmen launched various educational, charitable, cultural and political organisations and the committees they set up were considered as enlightened and tolerant by Roman Catholic inhabitants of the town.

This tradition, a form of self-government, began with the Belfast Incorporated Charitable Society, known as the Poor House – 'a noble proof of the general philanthropy which prevailed in Belfast' – which was first opened on Donegall Street in 1774.[3] The soup kitchen started in the late eighteenth century was due to the 'liberal efforts of the inhabitants for the poorer classes'.[4]

The high moral tone prevailing among the well-to-do in the town in the late eighteenth century is perfectly captured by the historian George Benn writing a generation later:

> It was recommended that gentlemen and ladies religiously dedicated their winnings at cards to the benefit of the poor ... that invitations to dinner or evening parties be less frequent ... and that all saddle and carriage horses be put upon half their allowance of oats.[5]

A committee for a maternity hospital and another for the Belfast Academy were set up in 1785. A fever hospital with more than 200 beds was also established. The House of Industry, or Poor House, began life in 1809, and the House of Correction (a prison-cum-workhouse) was founded in 1817. From 1815 a Society for Discountenancing Vice distributed low-priced religious books and tracts

and also promoted a Bible Society and a Ladies' Bible
Association. In 1802 a Belfast Sunday School was
founded; liberal in its principles, the school did not
discriminate on grounds of religion and catered for no
fewer than 700 children. The Belfast Reading Society
became the Belfast Society for Promoting Knowledge,
and a library was established which was later to move to
the Linen Hall, today a magnificent building facing the
City Hall. A Belfast Literary Society was also founded,
but George Benn noted that:

> there is little taste in Belfast for the fine arts ... It has been
> said to have meddled too much with politics to have
> attended to such affairs and that a greater relish for literary
> pursuits might modify this political spirit.[6]

Liberté, Egalité, Sécularité

The lack of formal outlets for political expression
explains the attraction for middle-class people of the
Volunteers, a Protestant militia which, set up during the
American War of Independence to protect the country
against possible invasion by France, slowly transformed
itself into a nationalist body. The powerful influence
exerted by the French Revolution in Belfast stemmed in
large part from the frustration caused by Dublin's
monopoly of political power and a resulting feeling of
powerlessness in Ulster. The Northern Whig Club was
established in 1789 and the United Irishmen, formed in
1791, were composed above all of members of the
Protestant mercantile and professional classes of Belfast
and Dublin who had been influenced by the European
Enlightenment through the Scottish universities. Ulster
Presbyterians, and particularly those who lived in
Belfast, were the most radical elements of eighteenth-
century dissent. They were excluded from public office
and their church was penalised. They first supported the
Northern Whig Club and then a new project of a secret
society in order to achieve the Rights of Man.[7] The
occasion of their first public demonstration was to

celebrate the anniversary of the fall of the Bastille in 1791. This took the form of a popular festival which attracted large crowds into the streets. Among the slogans on the banners paraded on that 14th of July were 'Where Liberty is, there is my Country' and 'Superstitious Jealousy, the Cause of the Irish Bastille; let us unite and destroy it'.[8] Volunteers and citizens formed a procession through the town carrying portraits of the American and French revolutionaries Franklin and Mirabeau, 'displaying by their works as well as by their action, the most excessive joy and sympathy at the efforts of the French people' according to George Benn. An address to the National Assembly in Paris was adopted by the crowd, but even at this stage all references to Catholic emancipation were dropped 'in the interests of unanimity'.[9]

In July 1792 the French Revolution was celebrated with similar rejoicings by a crowd bearing numerous flags, which must have been the first tricolours to be seen in Ireland, and Benn claimed that 'The French Revolution has nowhere been celebrated with more pomp, more pure sincerity and genuine satisfaction than this town.'[10] The optimism of the early 1790s disappeared, however, following the declaration of war between Britain and France and the failure of Wolfe Tone's ill-fated Bantry Bay expedition in association with the French, and Belfast became the centre of anti-republican repression. The *Northern Star* office was ransacked by the military in 1797, and by June of that year 103 of the United Irishmen's leaders were in jail.

It is often assumed that the anti-Protestant aspect of the peasant rebellion at the end of the eighteenth century turned the radicalism of Belfast Protestants into conservatism.[11] But from the outset the difficulty of including Catholic emancipation in the United Irishmen's programme shows that anti-Catholicism predated the Wexford massacres, in which hundreds of Catholic peasants were killed by the Volunteers in retaliation for the murder of a few members of the

Protestant gentry. Two centuries later some loyalists nevertheless cite events in Belfast at the time of the French Revolution as proof of the radicalism of the Presbyterian tradition. In summer 1987 the sacrifice of Willie Nelson, a United Irishman who was arrested and hanged, was commemorated by a loyalist band parade. The demonstration was organised by the Ulster Young Unionist Culture Committee whose intention it is to make this an annual event 'since we believe the 1798 rebellion to be an important and wholesome part of the Ulster Presbyterian heritage'.[12] It should be noted, however, that these Young Unionists prefer to dwell on the anti-Catholic character of the French Revolution rather than Wolfe Tone's project of uniting all religious denominations.

The local historian Brendan Clifford has argued that 'Belfast participated in the French Revolution as no other town outside France did,'[13] and that, although its political life was stifled because it was a pocket borough controlled by Lord Chichester, by the late eighteenth century the town was vibrant and bustling:

> The civic energy of Belfast could not be harnessed to the Corporation because the Corporation had to be preserved as Chichester's pocket electorate ... So it used other channels to express its politics. The French Revolution was one such channel, and the celebrations of July 1791 and '92 showed that the town was whole-heartedly behind the events in Paris. Belfast was entirely bourgeois in its morals ... If the National Assembly could have been located in Belfast, it would have had its perfect environment. The social texture of Paris was too rich for it. Under the disturbing influence of the *sans culottes*, the French bourgeoisie lost their equipoise, and embarked on the exciting, bewildering year known ever since as the Reign of Terror.[14]

Belfast, however, had no *sans culottes* and 'the possibility of a social rupture between the top and the bottom was warded off by a well-conducted, paternalistic local Poor Law'. Clifford sees the Terror as caused by the refusal of the French Catholic Church, under the influence of Rome, to accept a civil constitiution for the clergy, and he is also quite happy to dispose of what he sees as the myth of idyllic relations between Catholics and Protestants at the time. The United Irishmen might have demanded the emancipation of Catholics in general, but they also rejoiced in the fact that in France the monastic orders were dissolved, the Jesuits expelled from the country and churches all over the land were turned into 'Temples of Reason'.

Economics and Politics

After the failure of the United Irishmen's rising in 1798 and the Act of Union with Britain that followed it the Ascendancy ensured that Belfast was kept on the fringes of Irish political affairs. The town's economics became its politics. In Belfast the great names of the nineteenth century were Harland and Wolff, 'shipbuilders to the world'. Only when the Home Rule crisis burst did political leaders of some stature – Carson and Craig – first appear in Belfast.[15] As before, the town's middle class preferred to compete for a seat on the Harbour Commission rather than one on the council. In the South the reverse was the case: every single economic development or problem became automatically linked to the major political question of the day, whether Catholic Emancipation, the Repeal of the Act of Union or Home Rule. Land agitation, social unrest and the middle classes' aspiration for greater power all became inextricably linked to political issues. Whatever criticisms might be made of the nationalists, they provided a remarkable training ground and gave the South such great political and trade union leaders as O'Connell, Parnell, Connolly, Larkin and de Valera.

While Dublin developed a major political forum based on the issue of nationalism, Belfast, although integrated economically with the United Kingdom and the British Empire, received only minor ripples from the mainland's major political conflicts. The only occasion when Belfast was a political arena of consequence was at the time of the United Irishmen and the French Revolution. Thereafter it was bypassed by the movement for parliamentary reform, turned its back on Chartism, ignored the development of the Labour Party (though not of trade unionism) and had nothing to do with the suffragette movement. Even the two world wars, in spite of official rhetoric, did not bring about major changes of attitude. The Second World War, as we shall see, was a time when Ulster had to prove its loyalty, but here it did not become the 'people's war' of democracy against fascism as it was elsewhere in the United Kingdom. The most immediate consequence of isolation was political stagnation and this meant that Belfast could not provide a training ground for political leaders.

Let us not beat about the bush. We are trying to understand the present conflict in the city and, I suppose, the North in general. The troubles loom large in any incursion into the past, but political history will not necessarily help us much in this respect. The pattern of conquerors who take the losers' place and then proceed to organise their control over the vanquished is by no means unique to Northern Ireland.

Political life in the city lay dormant until it reacted to the growth and development of the nationalist movement in the South with the movement for the repeal of the Penal Laws and later for repeal of the Act of Union. By then, having grown into a fully fledged industrial city which looked to the east for its prosperity and considered itself as the capital of the industrial and Protestant North, Belfast felt threatened by the budding Catholic and nationalist movement in the South. But instead of engaging in a real dialogue the two sides spoke to each other in different languages, the South's political and the North's economic. Again and again it is very clear that the South offered political arguments to support its case – what was at stake was its political and cultural independence – while the North responded with economic arguments. A perfect example of this was the reaction of Henry Cooke, the founding father of

Presbyterian fundamentalism, to Daniel O'Connell's visit to Belfast. 'The Liberator', who everywhere else in Ireland was greeted as the messiah, had to be protected from angry crowds in Belfast, and Cooke justified this hostility by recalling the economic miracle that was Belfast:

> Our town was merely a village. But what a glorious sight it now presents ... new streets and public buildings – numbers of new manufactories ... signs of increasing prosperity ... and to what cause? Is it not the free intercourse which the Union enables us to enjoy with England and Scotland – to that extension of our general commerce which we enjoy through that channel? ... I see the genius of industry ... which looks down upon our lovely town ... accompanied by the genius of Protestantism.[16]

This exchange – for it is hardly a dialogue – in different languages has gone on virtually uninterrupted until the present. As we shall see in Chapter 7, it took place in the early years of this century between James Connolly, the revolutionary leader, and William Walker, the cautious Belfast trade unionist who used his version of municipal socialism to try to squash his opponent's impetuous nationalism. It should be emphasised that this was not originally a dialogue between Unionism and nationalism but between North and South, because until the 1920s the core of Irish Unionism was the Anglo-Irish Ascendancy whose base was in Dublin. The struggle between the Ascendancy and the nationalists was very much a political one, with both sides fighting for power and influence over the peasantry and the urban middle class. Incredible as it may seem today, the Dublin Anglo-Irish did not use the strength of the Northern economy to reinforce their case, and this economic prowess only became the main political argument once the battle in the South had clearly been lost by the Ascendancy and the struggle over Home Rule had moved to the North. This explains why the loyalists' case sometimes appears somewhat dull and dreary, rather like a piece of planning for an industrial development area, whereas Southern nationalism was always flamboyant, full of political rhetoric, Gaelic cultural revivals and theatrical premieres of international importance.

The current impasse in Northern Ireland is not, fundamentally, due to political developments but to economic change, although the troubles, the fall of Stormont and the Anglo-Irish Agreement all play their role. Because of the collapse of the major industrial power-houses of the city it is no longer possible to present Belfast as a model of economic prosperity. Despite problems caused by the inter-war recession, the Unionist establishment was until the 1960s able to deliver the goods to the majority of the working-class population in the North. This is no longer the case. It cannot now guarantee employment for its own people, let alone to the Catholics who are demanding equal job opportunities. The problem has been made more acute by the relative prosperity of the Republic in recent years, and Belfast Protestants are no longer able to look disparagingly at the South's economy as they did in the past. Protestant nationalism, in the circumstances, is bound to become more 'cultural' and more strident, and will inevitably come to look more and more like the cultural nationalism of the South in the early decades of the century.

The Rise of Industry

Ireland had a thriving woollen industry until protecttionist legislation passed by the Westminster parliament in the late eighteenth century destroyed it. A century before this the repeal of the Edict of Nantes and the expulsion of the Huguenots from France in 1685, however, had given a major boost to another local textile industry. Huguenot refugees led by Louis Crommelin (who gave his name to the Crumlin Road) settled in Lisburn, bringing with them their technical skill in the growing of flax and manufacture of linen, and also their marketing experience and capital. A linen

market was organised in Belfast in 1720. In the
eighteenth century a contemporary observer described
the slopes running down to the Lagan as white with
bleaching linen. Bleaching was a chemical process
demanding a large capital outlay and the bleachers soon
became employers, the weavers and spinners employees.
A banking system developed to facilitate investment and
development, and a canal was built to ease the transport
of goods to Lough Neagh. In 1757 the population was
8,500, and by 1782 it had grown to 13,000. The 120
inmates of the Poor House were engaged in handloom
weaving and spinning. Children trained in the Poor
House were used in the cotton mills as spinners, and the
introduction of the cotton industry to the town was in fact
the result of hard Presbyterian thinking about how to
best to employ the young people lodged in the Poor
House.

By the middle of the eighteenth century the twin
pillars of Belfast industry, linen and shipbuilding, were
established. Linen-spinning and weaving were above all
domestic industries carried on in farmhouses and
cottages in the surrounding countryside, and Belfast was
primarily the organising centre and market for linen.
The foundation stone of the great Linen Hall was laid in
1784.

Thomas Mulholland introduced mechanised flax-
spinning to the town in the early nineteenth century, and
the success of the linen industry acted as a spur for other
activities – glassworks, potteries and ropeworks. In 1800,
just before the Act of Union with Britain, Belfast was the
fifth largest town in Ireland, with a number of fine
Georgian buildings, although few of these survived the
Victorian expansion of the city. In 1815 Belfast had
30,000 people, and by 1841 the population had more than
doubled to 70,000. When Queen Victoria came to the
throne in 1837 Belfast was an important industrial and
commercial city known as 'the Irish Liverpool' or 'a clean
Manchester', and the period which followed was one of
rapid growth in which the modern city took shape. Both

housing conditions and industry were typical of British
industrial cities of the period. Approximately 70 per cent
of the labour force in linen, the staple industry, was
female. The set-up looked harmonious: shipbuilding
provided jobs for the men and the linen mills work for
their wives and daughters.

The harbour was the city's most important feature and
was constantly improved. In 1843 the Long Bridge was
replaced by the Queen's Bridge, across which, in later
decades, thousands of men flocked to and from the
Harland and Wolff shipyard on foot, by bicycle or in
human swarms clinging to the trams. Today the journey
from the city centre to the shipyards is quite different.
Men no longer walk or cycle to work any more, they drive.
The late afternoon is now a long traffic jam, which is
much less spectacular than the armies of men hanging
onto trams or weaving in and out on their bicycles who
were once prominent in the opening shots of films about
Belfast.

George Benn, for a time the official historian of the
town, divided Belfast's population in the early nineteenth century into Scots, English and Irish. The most
important group was composed of descendants of the
Scots; the English were established in Malone, known
today as South Belfast, the most prosperous area of the
city. The Irish, the poorest inhabitants, lived in a hilly
district in the south-western part of the parish.[17] In the
early eighteenth century the native Irish were forced to
live outside the city walls by the English and Scottish
settlers and were concentrated on the west bank of the
Lagan from where they later moved to the northern and
western parts of the town. Should this exclusion of
Catholics strike English or other foreign readers as a
particularly outrageous example of Irish religious
discrimination it might perhaps be recalled that Jews
were not allowed to be Freemen of the City of London,
and so could not own property, live or run a business
there until 1832, and that in France this sort of
discrimination was not swept away until the Revolution.

The denial of residential and commercial rights to 'strangers' was common to nearly all European cities until relatively recently and by no means restricted to those societies which are now believed to have a history of discrimination on racial or religious grounds.

The majority of Belfast's poor when the first Poor House was opened were Catholics and Catholic districts always contained the worst slums, but the Poor House did not discriminate on grounds of religion and '[the children] walk on the Sabbath day, hand in hand, to the respective houses of worship,' and received donations from all religious denominations. In other respects, however, Belfast in the late eighteenth century was not the worst place in Ireland in which Catholics might live. In 1784 the Belfast Volunteers marched to the opening of the new Catholic church where they contributed £84 to the building fund, a gesture often quoted as an example of how relations between Protestants and Catholics might have been. Clifford's caveats about the difficult relations between the two religions should, however, be taken into account, as it is very easy for present-day observers to try to reconstruct an old Ireland free of sectarian tensions.

Until the early nineteenth century the overwhelming majority of Belfast's population was Protestant, and the city's historian was proud of the fact. In 'genius and disposition' Belfast's citizens shared none of those carefree and light-hearted attitudes

> which the common voice has attributed to the Irish race; they are a plodding people, cool, dry, deliberate ... They are totally different from the prodigal and submissive inhabitants of other parts of this kingdom.[18]

In 1808 there were 4,000 Catholics in Belfast, 16 per cent of the population; by 1834 there were 19,712 Catholics out of a population of 60,813. The Catholic proportion of the town's inhabitants grew regularly until it reached 34 per cent in the 1850s; by 1926, however, it had fallen to 23 per cent because, although Catholics continued to come to the city from the South and West, they were outnumbered by Protestant newcomers from the mainland. It was only during and after the Second World War that the Catholic proportion of the population began to rise again due to wartime employment opportunities and the creation of a better welfare system after 1945.

In the 1830s Belfast began to grow rapidly. Industry needed labour and Catholics from the South and West of Ireland filled the vacancies in the linen trade. Within a few years thousands of rural Catholics had poured into the city. These immigrants were not townsfolk and were bound to clash with typical Protestant Belfast artisans, whose speech, industrial habits and work ethic were the opposite to those of the 'uncouth intruders whom they regarded as competitors for their jobs and their homes'.[19] Most Protestant workers at that time were members of the Orange Order whose aim of uniting loyalists of all classes is summed up in this popular verse:

> Let not the poor man hate the rich,
> Nor rich on poor look down
> But each join each true Orange Order
> For God and for the Crown.[20]

In the mid-nineteenth century the rural population flooded into the city in the wake of the Famine, while iron shipbuilding was established and the linen industry became mechanised. Roads and railways were built and developed into a proper network linking the city with its hinterland.

In 1832 Belfast was a town of some 50,000 people. The first shipbuilder was William Ritchie, a Scot who brought skilled labour with him from the Clyde, and in 1820 launched Ireland's first steamboat. Edward Harland, a former apprentice of the great engineer Robert Stephenson, arrived in Belfast from Glasgow in 1854 and entered into partnership with Gustav Wolff who had been born in Hamburg, educated in Liverpool and later moved to Belfast. Their names are as indissolubly linked with Belfast's history as those of Rolls and Royce are with the history of the motor car or Rodgers and Hammerstein with that of the American musical. Their initials are still on the shipyard cranes and are the first thing to welcome you to the city and the last to bid you farewell.

Through family connections Harland and Wolff secured orders from the Bibby Line and built eighteen ocean-going vessels for the Liverpool company; Belfast, it should never be forgotten, was part of the Mersey-Lagan-Clyde industrial triangle, part and parcel of a much bigger industrial complex. The public park on Queen's Island was taken over for shipbuilding. In 1861 the company employed 500 men, in 1865 some 900, in 1870 no fewer than 2,400 and by 1900 a staggering 9,000. The 'wee yard', Workman and Clark, also became world-famous. In the second half of the nineteenth century five major docks and basins were opened, marshy land was reclaimed and the industrial landscape of the city with its massive cranes, gantries and storage sheds thus created.

The Golden Age

Between 1835 and 1850 Belfast's population doubled to 90,000, but this was only the beginning of the success story. In the next fifty years the population would increase fourfold and a minor port would develop into a major one. Shipbuilding, starting from scratch, would challenge the world's leading yards. In 1852 there was one power loom in Belfast; ten years later there were 6,000. The linen industry, which imported its flax from northern Europe and Russia, boomed in the 1870s, and engineering developed to supply the needs of the linen industry.

The speed of industrial development was such that it was seen by many Presbyterians as nothing less than an economic miracle. Raw materials were almost non-existent, the port had to be reclaimed from the lough and the town's geographical position was unfavourable. Even many of the skilled workers had to be imported from Britain. Against all the odds, Belfast grew and thrived. Who else but the chosen people could have achieved such a miracle?

In 1900 Belfast was 350,000 strong. Wealth continued to move to the south of the city, towards Malone, Lisburn and Stranmillis. The residential districts were and still are separated from the centre by a green belt comprised of the Botanic Gardens, Queen's University and Methodist College. Science, education and nature were conducive to wealth, so industry and commerce in their turn had to encourage science, education and nature. Middle-class families organised the education of their sons and, to a lesser extent, of their daughters. Queen's University was established in 1848, followed in 1859 by the Victoria College for young women. Belfast High School, Victoria, Methodist and Campbell colleges were for Protestants; their Catholic counterparts were Saint Malachy's and Saint Mary's.

Strong and wealthy, the city came to feel more and more that it was the capital of a self-contained region, the Protestant industrial North. It had been raised to the status of a city in 1888 and its leaders wanted to show that they were wealthy and powerful. Unfortunately, not a great deal survives architecturally from Belfast's nineteenth-century heyday, but one or two gems are left. Foremost amongst these is a magnificent pub, the Crown on Great Victoria Street, a model of intricate decoration described as 'indisputably the crown of Victorian pubs in Ireland, and many would say in the British Isles'.[21] Robinson and Cleaver, the department store, provides another fine example of Victorian gothic. The City Hall was built in 1905; massive and dignified with its Portland stone, corner towers and soaring domes, it says to the world: 'We are rich and powerful and we are here to stay.' How was it possible, one can ask with the benefit of hindsight, that nationalist political leaders could ignore the political statement implicit in the City Hall's architecture and think nothing of dismantling it as if it were just another Martello tower built to keep the French at bay?

At the beginning of the twentieth century Belfast was at the height of its commercial and industrial power, and proud of it; the spirit of the town at the time can be caught in a guide published in 1902. Pride in industry rears its head again and again: 'Belfast as a town has no ancient history and does not lay claim to remote origin like so many towns in Ireland. Its record is simply one of industrial progress.'

Belfast was proud to be young in much the same way that American cities like Chicago also developed a patronising attitude to old-fashioned Europe, which was seen as pleasant but backward. The guide claims that Belfast, with the requisite number of success stories of self-made men, could be compared with an American city, and one feels the author thought that, like an American city, it also had a hinterland of wilderness where dangerous natives roamed in frontier territory. Down in the South, by contrast, they had ancestors, so they also had museums, galleries, bards and Georgian houses, but here in the North there 'is simply ... industrial progress'. Belfast boasted about its rapid economic growth, commercial spirit and the intelligence of its hard-working citizens: it was the capital of Ulster, the greatest commercial city in Ireland, 'the most progressive city in the country, possibly in the United Kingdom'.[22] This success story is attributed to the character and race of some of the town's inhabitants: 'Modern Belfast certainly owes very much of its reputation to the character and qualities of the Scottish settlers of King James's time...' If other peoples are mentioned they are 'settlers from all parts of the United Kingdom' and one suspects that Catholics are not included in 'the combination of races [which] has tended to produce a community not exceeded by that of any other part of the Empire for modern business aptitude'.

The guide goes on to describe the main industries and

emphasises what it sees as the harmonious division of labour in the city: shipbuilding and engineering for boys and men, linen and ropeworks for girls and women, 'and one may remark, *en passant*, that not the least of the causes of Belfast's success as a manufacturing centre is that its staple industries employ all the available members of the working man's family'. It was far from usual at this time for women's involvement in the workforce to be celebrated in this way, but unfortunately the picture of Janet going to the linen mill and John to the shipyard is inaccurate because, generally speaking, the wives and daughters of skilled Protestant workers were not in paid work. Women who went out to work were either unmarried or the wives of unskilled labourers whose wages were insufficient to keep the family going, in other words Catholics. In fact, John went off to work in the yard and Maureen to the mill. They never met and so never married.

In 1906 wages were on average between 20 and 25 per cent higher in Belfast than in rural areas of Ulster, and the income of skilled workers was on a par with their counterparts on the British mainland. Labourers' wages, however, were lower than elsewhere in the United Kingdom. In the first decade of the century occupations were, broadly speaking, distributed just as they were in a British industrial city like Bradford or Newcastle: three-quarters of those employed worked in manufacturing industry, one-twelfth in domestic service and one-twentieth in the professions. In 1910 Belfast certainly looked much more like Leeds than Dublin. It was the world's major linen centre, and the city had more spindles within its boundaries than any other country in the world. It was also, of course, the industry's commercial centre, housing the offices and warehouses of flax, yarn and linen merchants.

Engineering was above all devoted to the production of linen machinery, but the tobacco industry also needed plant and Mollins manufactured internationally famous processing machinery which was exported to Russia,

Belgium, Germany and France. The core of Belfast's prosperity, shipbuilding, linen and engineering, depended on the link with Britain and the Empire. These three staple industrial activities employed 70,000 people in 1912, more than half of all industrial workers. The skills developed in textile engineering were useful in marine engineering, and vice versa, and there was considerable cross-fertilisation between the city's industries. Motor cars, bicycles, soap and candles were also produced locally, and William Black was quite correct to write in the 1960s that, 'One gets the impression that the Belfast of 1910 was a good deal more self-sufficient than the Belfast of today,'[23] but this was also true of most sizeable British cities. With the accelerating pace of technological development and the consequent growing scale of investment necessary, however, the only industries which could survive were those suitable for large-scale production, that is to say linen and shipbuilding. The other industries which survived in Belfast were those like brick-making which were protected from competition by transport costs. The First World War added to the city's prosperity. The yards built both merchant- and warships, engineering was in large part turned over to munitions and linen received a boost through its use to make wings for biplanes.

Crash

Then came the slump of 1921 and Belfast, like the other great industrial cities of the United Kingdom, suffered severely. During the 1930s international competition became more intense and the recession hit the city even harder than that of the early 1920s; by the winter of 1939 there were 20,000 unemployed in Belfast. In shipbuilding employment fell from 20,000 in 1924 to 2,000 in 1933, when Harland and Wolff did not launch a single vessel, and Workman and Clark went out of business altogether in 1934. Employment in engineering only regained the levels of the 1920s in the late 1930s, due primarily to diversification, when Short Brothers and Harland and Wolff combined to set up an aircraft industry, Short and Harland. The recovery in ship-building was much slower, and the 1929 level of employment was not reached again until 1939 when preparations for the impending war were well under way. Linen, however, never regained its position and in the summer of 1938 more than half the industry's workers were unemployed as a result of competition from cotton and artificial fibres.

The 1930s were an important turning-point, a sort of dress-rehearsal for the crisis of the 1970s. Until then the story of the city had been one of continuous growth. Belfast was seen as 'the product of human endeavour working upon the natural advantages of a well-chosen site'.[24] It was a market for agricultural products and textiles, a major manufacturing centre, the only great industrial town in Ireland. The linen industry put a great deal of money in circulation and there was plenty of opportunity for the Protestant virtues of thrift and enterprise to mani-fest themselves. Ulster agriculture also helped foster industrial development as tenant farmers in the province enjoyed greater security of tenure than those elsewhere in Ireland, and their savings helped create capital which was invested in industry. There was therefore less of the abso-lute dependence on the land characteristic of the South and West of Ireland. Ulster was the most prosperous part of Ireland and the 1930s were the first major setback in this history of uninterrupted growth. In the worst years of the depression a quarter of the working population, over 50,000 people, were unemployed.

The worst effects of the recession were slightly offset by the growth of service industries. The wholesale and retail trades, professional services, education, govern-ment and administration employed 80,000 people in 1926 and 100,000 in 1937. This growth foreshadowed developments after the Second World War when the increase in employment in the service industries would be the major positive feature in the economic life of the city.

In fact, Belfast's major industries never really recovered from the inter-war recession, and the Second World War now looks like a temporary reprieve in a process of inexorable decline. Ships were built, of course, for the both the Royal and Merchant Navy. Short and Harland's major contribution to the war effort was the famous Stirling bomber, of which more than 1,300 were built, but production came to an abrupt end in November 1945. In fact the Northern Ireland economy was slow to adapt to the war, and a year after war was declared the unemployment rate in the province was as bad as it had been in 1932, the worst year of the recession, while in Great Britain it had fallen by half. The linen industry collapsed, unable to import raw flax from Russia.

Post-War Decline

In 1967 linen and shipbuilding between them provided only one-tenth of all employment in the city, and employed 15,000 people, half the 1952 total. Attempts to start up new industries have not reduced overall unemployment. New factories making computers, tape recorders and drilling equipment have slightly offset the decline in heavy engineering. Total employment grew from 150,000 in 1901 to 260,000 in the 1960s because of the growth in services. In 1901 only 5,000 people in Belfast worked for central or local government, a figure which by 1967 had increased to 22,000, 8 per cent of all those employed in the city.

Between 1961 and 1968 employment in manufacturing industry fell from 106,000 to 92,000 while employment in the service industries rose from 133,000 to 145,000. Shipbuilding reached its post-war peak in the mid-1960s and then collapsed; the last great passenger liner to be built in Belfast, the *Canberra*, was launched in 1960. Due to intense foreign competition Harland and Wolff was reorganised to specialise in the production of large bulk carriers, especially oil tankers, just at the time that the market for such ships was about to collapse.

In 1972 male unemployment in Belfast was 7.7 per cent; by 1981 this had grown to 21.3 per cent, with local pockets approaching 50 per cent. High unemployment is a social disaster wherever it occurs, but its effects are much worse in Belfast because it makes ethnic rivalries more acute. In 1981 no less than 72.4 per cent of those in work were employed in the service industries, but the dramatic increase in this type of employment was not sufficient to offset the loss of jobs in other sectors of the economy. It is the end of an era for Ulster, which was once the most prosperous province of Ireland, and also for Belfast, at one time the fastest growing city in the United Kingdom. Northern Ireland is now reduced to the status of a minor region: it has just 3 per cent of the UK's population and produces 2 per cent of its gross national product. It is the region with the lowest per capita income, the highest rate of unemployment and the highest rate of outward migration.

The decline shows no sign of slowing up, and crisis and decay are the most frequently used words in any discussion of Northern Ireland's economy. After the rapid growth of the 1960s industrial output fell in the 1970s. Industrial employment has fallen by around 40 per cent in the last ten years. Some industries, like synthetic fibres, have virtually disappeared. In many ways Belfast has simply been a victim of the global slump, but its decline was more severe than that of other cities and its recovery much weaker. Manufacturing employment has fallen continually, and in the mid-1980s the province was losing manufacturing jobs at the rate of 1 or 2 per cent a year, and a combination of the decline in overall manufacturing output (17 per cent) and the rise in labour productivity (41 per cent) accounts for the greater part of the decline in employment.[25] Some industries – aircraft, motor vehicles and parts – have shown signs of recovery, while others – shipbuilding, clothing and chemicals – are now in terminal decline. Meanwhile the Republic continues to attract foreign investment and, despite certain problems and weaknesses, its economy increasingly looks more attractive than the North's.

Throughout the 1980s the policies of the Thatcher governments had harmful and dramatic consequences for Belfast: reluctant to subsidise industries in difficulty, they also did their best to halt the expansion of the public sector, a particularly damaging policy in Belfast. Employment in the public services is now stable, and for the first time there has recently been a fall in the number of people employed in private services. All major forms of employment in Belfast are either stagnant or in decline. What went wrong?

Notes

1   E. Estyn Evans, 'The Geographical Setting' in J.C. Beckett and R.E. Glassock (eds), *Belfast – The Origin and Growth of an Industrial City*, London 1967.

2   George Benn, *The History of the Town of Belfast*, Belfast 1823, p. 113.

3   Ibid., p. 106.

4   Ibid.

5   Ibid., 1890 edition, p. 29.

6   Ibid., p. 128.

7   Marianne Elliott, *Partners in Revolution: The United Irishmen and France*, New Haven and London 1982, p. 21.

8   Brendan Clifford, *Belfast in the French Revolution*, Belfast 1989, pp. 60-1.

9   Elliott, op. cit., p. 22.

10   Benn, op. cit., 1823 edition, p. 59.

11   Thomas Pakenham, *The Year of Liberty, The Story of the Great Irish Rebellion of 1798*, London 1969.

12   *Newsletter*, 5 October 1987.

13   Clifford, op. cit., p. 12.

14   Ibid., pp. 5–11.

15   Alvin Jackson, *The Ulster Party, Irish Unionists in the House of Commons, 1884–1911*, Oxford 1989.

16   Jonathon Bardon, *An Illustrated History of Belfast*, Belfast 1982.

17   Benn, 1823 edition, p. 197.

18   Ibid., p. 199.

19   Paddy Devlin, *Yes, We Have No Bananas – Outdoor Relief in Belfast 1920–1939*, p. 17.

20   Ibid., p. 18.

21   Mark Girouard, *Victorian Pubs*, New Haven and London 1984, p. 243.

22   *A Guide to Belfast and the Counties of Down and Antrim*, Belfast 1902, p. 7.
23   William Black, 'Industrial Change in the Twentieth Century' in Beckett and Glassock (eds), op. cit., p. 161.
24   Beckett in Beckett and Glassock (eds), op. cit.
25   Bob Rowthorn, 'Northern Ireland, An Economy in Crisis' in Paul Teague (ed.), *Beyond the Rhetoric: Politics, the Economy and Social policy in Northern Ireland*, London 1987, p. 113.

2   Yes, We Have No Jobs

The debate about the decline of Belfast's economy is part and parcel of the fundamental political conflict. For some, the troubles are the cause of the economic crisis. For others, economic decline is the main reason for the troubles. Any comparison between Belfast and Dublin inevitably raises the question of whether partition was favourable or unfavourable in economic terms. Would a united Ireland be a boon for Belfast's economy or another, possibly final, nail in its coffin?

Take the question of subsidies, or 'British tax-payers' money' as some people insist on calling them, which are approximately twice as high in Northern Ireland as in other depressed areas of the United Kingdom. Shorts is widely considered a successful company, but it has lost money consistently since the mid-1970s. During the mid-1980s Harland and Wolff received an average subsidy of £8,000 a year for each employee, almost sufficient to meet the company's entire wage and salary bill. It would be much cheaper to make redundancy payments and close the site – nothing much is left anyway. But you do not close down a symbol. Who would dream of closing the Eiffel Tower, the Empire State Building or Tower Bridge? The Belfast equivalent of these buildings which symbolise their cities are the huge cranes where 'Belfast created such sea monsters with its own hands' and which still cause a twinge of pride in the hearts of Belfastmen and women.[1] The conclusion is obvious: the city's main industries depend on the British and living standards would fall dramatically if they closed. The economist Bob Rowthorn has drawn the harsh but accurate conclusion that 'Northern Ireland now resembles a vast workhouse in which most of the inmates are engaged in servicing or controlling each other.'[2]

The expansion of public services in Northern Ireland during the post-war period was largely funded by Whitehall. A *Financial Times* special issue on Northern Ireland confirms this view of the province as a 'dependent economy': its economic output is static while that of the rest of the United Kingdom has been rising; government spending is equivalent to 70 per cent of its gross domestic product; more than 40 per cent of all those in employment work in the public sector.[3]

Matters are made still worse by the job structure. Rising unemployment has its harshest effects on manual workers who already live close to the poverty line, but at the same time the standard of living of those who have managed to keep their jobs has risen sharply since the early 1970s, in part because housing is much cheaper in the North than in Britain while civil service salaries are the same as those elsewhere in the United Kingdom. This goes a long way to explaining why 'Belfast is buzzing' and allows the *Belfast Telegraph* to observe that 'Anyone returning to the city after a few years' absence cannot fail to be impressed by the new vibrancy of the shops and places of entertainment.'[4] The number of Catholic and Protestant public service professionals is on the rise, but so is unemployment and poverty in both communities.

The situation is much worse for Catholics, however, as the unemployment rate is 2.5 per cent higher among them. About one male Protestant in ten is employed directly or indirectly in the policing of the province, so should peace break out the brunt of any cuts in the security forces would be borne above all by the majority community. By 1988 Shorts, with a workforce of 7,800, had overtaken Harland and Wolff as the largest non-government employer in Northern Ireland, the third being Dupont with 1,500 in Derry. Out of a total manufacturing workforce of 100,000 in the province only 28,000 live in Belfast. Meanwhile no fewer than 200 restaurants opened in Belfast between 1983 and 1988, and Sunday 4 October 1987 was an historic day: pubs were allowed to open on the sabbath. Paisley and a few Free Presbyterians demonstrated in front of those pubs which took advantage of the relaxation of the law, but most pubs in the centre of town are now open on Sundays.

There is, of course, disagreement about the basic reasons for economic decline and whether this should be attributed to partition or the war of attrition waged by the paramilitaries. Violence is always condemned by the SDLP and others as a job-destroying process, and whenever there is a murder or explosion, statements and speeches are made attacking the 'so-called friends of the people' who destroy factories and shops, thus creating even more hardship for the populace. What is more surprising is the general agreement in Belfast on anti-Tory policy. If economics were the decisive issue in Belfast the most left-wing candidates would be elected with overwhelming majorities. Rumours of the privatisation of Harland and Wolff, Shorts or the local electricity board were met with a general outcry, with leaders of all the trade unions and political parties, including those which might be expected to back Conservative policies, joining in the condemnation. Sinn Fein is not in favour of the withdrawal of British money: 'Brits out' apparently means 'British troops out', not British money. Ken Maginnis of the Official Unionist Party stridently insists that public subsidies must continue; the trouble, he says, is that 'we' have no government of our own. The Northern Ireland Office is out of touch with public feeling, Maginnis insists, and does not fight for the province's interests – 'We are ruled by dictate.'[5] Sounding more like a caricature of a militant shop steward than someone who sits on the Tory benches at Westminster, he warns that all enterprises targeted for privatisation have 100 per cent union membership:

'We will fight.' Peter Robinson of the Democratic
Unionist Party represents the working-class East
Belfast, home of both Harland and Wolff and Shorts, and
argues that privatisation might make sense in the
South-East of England but not in Belfast, although why
this should be is not made clear. After making a wildly
anti-colonialist statement – 'the profits of these companies have in the past been lifted and taken to the
mainland' – the withdrawal of British subsidies is seen
as tantamount to political withdrawal by Great Britain.

So industry is crumbling and unemployment rising,
but meanwhile many people in Belfast are doing well
with jobs that are heavily subsidised by public money. If
Northern Ireland is part of the United Kingdom,
however, its economic predicament cannot be discussed
as if it were a foreign country, as it is simply one of
several depressed areas. If you are in love you don't count
the cost, as the French saying goes; if you start counting
it is because you are thinking of divorce. To argue that
Britain foots the bill for Belfast is only possible if the city
is not considered an integral part of the United Kingdom.

One of my pleasures in this valley of tears is to travel
from Belfast to London with notes issued by the Ulster
Bank. These notes are legal tender, but I have never been
able to pay my taxi fare without a long and lively
discussion with the driver, and in shops the manager
always has to be called to settle the issue. It would be
easier, I am sure, to pay with dollars or francs. For these
Londoners who question the validity of Ulster banknotes
any money sent to Belfast is a subsidy to a foreign
country.

Discrimination

Job discrimination lies at the heart of the underlying
conflict. Catholics in Northern Ireland do not see the
state as legitimate and so are not considered as bona fide
citizens by Protestants. Equal opportunity in the job
market is only a really pressing issue when the group in

question has become fully accepted as part of the body politic in the way that blacks were in the United States in the 1960s. In a slightly different way equal opportunity for women becomes a pressing issue if women's presence in the workplace is not casual or a transitory interval between school and marriage, in other words if women become 'citizens' in the workplace.

The arguments against affirmative action used by some Protestants are very similar to those used in France against Arab and African workers – the nationalist community is seen as a group of 'foreigners' to whom the country owes nothing. The entire history of welfare provision in Belfast has prepared people's minds for this type of exclusion,[6] so much so that Protestants who fell on hard times were also made to feel like outsiders. Winifred Campbell remembers how in the 1920s all the men except two in her street in the Shankill were on the dole and that prospective beneficiaries of the relief scheme, which provided employment on the roads for a few weeks, had to be interviewed. Between interviews one man's wife had a child, and the woman interviewer asked him: 'Why do you breed them when you can't feed them?'[7] The bitterness created by such remarks, the deliberate humiliation of the means test, was common to members of both religions, but there was an additional twist because in using the word 'breed' she spoke to this unemployed Protestant as he expected only Catholics could be addressed. Robert Harbinson had exactly the same feeling when he was evacuated from Belfast during the Second World War; the Protestants with whom they were billeted 'instead of treating us as good Orange brethren, they thought us social outcasts' and one woman in the village described her evacuees as so dirty that they might have been Catholics from the Free State.[8]

We have seen that a new town council was elected in 1842 after the passing of the Municipal Corporation Act. Most Catholics were too poor to qualify as electors and all 40 seats were won by the Conservatives, but the new council had a policy more akin to that of progressive Liberalism than that of the Conservative Party in mainland Britain. The council supported the 1847 Act which limited hours of work for women and children in textile mills to ten hours a day, and the 1850 Act which extended the ten-hour day to male workers.

In 1838 the government set up 130 Poor Law unions uniting the parishes of Ireland, each of which was to be governed by an elected Board of Guardians. A new workhouse was built in Belfast designed to accommodate 1,000 inmates; women were to do the domestic chores while the men broke stones or picked oakum. According to the Irish Poor Law Commissioners' rules, the work was to be sufficiently irksome to increase a desire to leave the workhouse, while the food would be inferior to that ordinarily eaten by the labouring classes in the neighbourhood. The population of Belfast's workhouse was further swollen by British Poor Law unions' habit of repatriating destitute Irish immigrants to Belfast as the most convenient port.[9]

From the different reports on the state of health of the poor in the United Kingdom it is clear that their lot was worse in Belfast than elsewhere. In the mid-nineteenth century the annual mortality rate in Great Britain was 1 in 50, while in Belfast it was 1 in 36. In the 1850s the Reverend Hanlon described the 'revolting, heart-rending spectacle' of urban misery in Belfast and described the city as a 'gate to perdition'. The Board of Guardians of the workhouse had even dismissed from their custody 'some unfortunate and guilty females', and he met a woman lying hungry and in rags who was adamant in her refusal to apply to the workhouse for assistance because 'she thinks liberty is a thrice glorious Goddess'.

Belfast's relative prosperity contrasted with the poverty and famine of the South and West of Ireland, however, and the comparison made it easy for employers to keep wages down. Linen was, as we have seen, the biggest employer in nineteenth-century Belfast, and despite Larkin's efforts at the beginning of the twentieth century there were no trade unions for women in the industry. Skilled men were relatively well paid, but at the turn of the century 68 per cent of the labour force in the industry was female and 26 per cent were young people under the age of eighteen. The boundary between employment and the workhouse was a very narrow one.

Of the 34 Poor Law Guardians about 30 were Unionists. Elections took place every three years and members of the business community had a double vote; the electoral register included householders but not lodgers. The Guardians were drawn mainly from the lower middle class and were strongly Calvinistic. They felt endowed with a mission: destitute or unemployed paupers were being punished by God for some sin they had committed, and they, the Guardians, were part of the wrath of God. After partition the situation became even worse, as the Guardians saw themselves as being in the front line of a war to maintain the Protestant majority and so were intent on preventing nationalists from receiving relief and instead concentrated their efforts on aiding the loyalist unemployed. The workhouse tests on destitution were rigidly applied and the Board earned an awesome reputation for its severity. In the face of sloth and fecklessness it was the Guardians' duty to discourage idleness. So much money was wasted on gambling and drink, but 'these people would make an effort to find work if they found that they could not get relief'.[10] All aspects of applicants' private lives were sifted through during interviews, and Catholics were told to ignore Church teaching about sex and contraception. Mrs Lily Coleman, who chaired the Outdoor Relief Committee in the early 1930s, is remembered for saying 'There is no poverty under the blanket.'[11]

Poor Law officers' reports provided information on religion and relations, as the relatives of paupers were threatened with court proceedings if they refused to maintain their kin. Applicants were pressed to sell their possessions to keep themselves as long as possible. Fares to enable the emigration of the poor were offered on terms that were almost impossible to refuse.[12] Applications for relief accompanied by a letter from Unionist headquarters, however, were almost always successful. The campaign to force 'unwanted' citizens out of Belfast never let up. The inevitable result was that the Catholic Church organised its own charitable work, and in the first four years of the 1920s the Saint Vincent de Paul Society helped more than eight people for every one relieved by the Poor Law Guardians.

Complaints about the relief system were so numerous that a civil servant came over from London and produced a damning report on the Belfast Board of Guardians. Whitehall announced that all relief schemes subsidised from its funds had to employ a ratio of one Catholic to two Protestants. This was, in effect, a quota system, and a strict one at that, but never came into effect as the Belfast Harbour Commissioners refused to accept funding on these terms: no Catholics were to be employed in the port.

As long as the job of denying Catholics relief was carried out efficiently the Stormont government made no attempt to interfere with the Belfast Board of Guardians. With the economic crisis of the 1930s unemployment and poverty began to affect a growing number of Protestants, but the Board stuck to its Calvinist guns and continued to regard any unemployed person as a sinner, irrespective of religion. In 1932 there were 50,000 unemployed in Belfast, half the total for Northern Ireland, and because of the long-term nature of that unemployment many Protestants were obliged to seek relief from the Poor Law Guardians and submit to humiliating enquiries into their personal lives. In Britain (where the Boards of Guardians had been abolished in 1929) the National Unemployed Workers' Movement had been organising marches and other forms of protest against the means test since the early 1920s, but the situation was worse in Belfast as the Guardians had for years been able to carry out their policy unhampered by any significant opposition; the average relief grant in Great Britain was £4 3s – in Belfast it was £2 10s.

In June 1927 William McMullen and Jack Beattie stood successfully for election as Guardians with the support of the trade unions and on a 'Labour' ticket (although they were not Labour Party candidates). The Unionist leadership began to feel that its special relationship with the loyalist working class was threatened and unsuccessfully pressed the Guardians to relax their policy. A new Poor Relief Act was resisted because, in the words of one of the Guardians, it represented a threat of extravagant expenditure as 'no period of residence [was] fixed as a condition ... thereby enabling a person just arrived from America or Cork to claim special relief'.[13] Tension reached a peak in October 1932 when 60,000 people from both religions demonstrated in Belfast, led by bands which, to avoid giving sectarian offence, played a neutral tune, 'Yes, We Have No Bananas'. This was followed by serious rioting in both the Shankill and the Falls, the building of barricades, deployment of troops, imposition of a curfew and the killing of demonstrators. Worried by the serious turn of events a delegation of businessmen and clergymen tried to persuade the Guardians to soften their policy, and for their pains were lectured by the chairman on the virtues of the work ethic and told that there were jobs available in the city but the poor refused to take them. Pressure within Belfast and from London was, however, such that relief rates were significantly increased.

The Belfast Board of Guardians was finally abolished in 1939, but they have left behind descendants who believe that if 'they' are given too much unemployment benefit or family income supplement they will swamp the province.

Intimidation

Report after report, survey after survey has made the same point – Roman Catholics in Northern Ireland have been discriminated against in employment, education, housing and in other areas.[14] The typical Protestant man in industry is skilled while the average Roman Catholic male is unskilled or unemployed. Roman Catholics, although they constitute one third of the economically active population, form the majority of the unemployed. Occupations which are strongly Protestant are generally male, while jobs in which Catholics are over-represented tend to be predominantly female. There is a not dissimilar pattern in education: Catholics, like women, tend to concentrate on the arts and social sciences, Protestants on science, engineering and other 'male' subjects.[15] The most striking statistics occur in the case of young people. In the sixteen to eighteen age group 18 per cent of Catholics and 17 per cent of Protestants are unemployed, but in the nineteen to twenty-four age bracket – when school and Youth Training Programmes are no longer applicable – the Protestant figure rises to just 19 per cent while the Catholic shoots up to 32 per cent. This is, of course, a major political problem and there is no apparent short- or medium-term solution.

There are constant complaints about the army and the police in the nationalist community, but relatively few about job discrimination. It seems to be taken for granted that discrimination is an unchangeable fact of life, with everything geared towards that end, and that there is no possibility of changing it through the Fair Employment Agency or any other body. Trade unions do not take up the issue, except in an abstract way. The problem is intractable. How on earth can the number of Catholic workers at Harland and Wolff be increased when there are so few Protestants left in the yard? Or take the example of an incident which took place in the 1980s in a large Belfast hotel, the staff of which is mostly Protestant. The hotel's Catholic employees received letters warning them that if they did not quit their jobs they would find themselves in serious trouble. Such letters are normally taken seriously in Belfast, and those hotel employees who received them quit their jobs – it is, after all, better to be on the dole than dead or seriously wounded. Letters of this sort go out from both camps, the killers deciding who is and who is not a legitimate target. In the Protestant hotel the Catholic barman is seen as being where he should not be and so becomes a 'legitimate target' of the Ulster Freedom Fighters, but by working in a Protestant establishment might well find himself serving an off-duty police officer and so become fair game for the IRA ... How can he win?

The Paris public transport network, like that in a number of other large cities, has a serious problem of attacks on drivers and guards. In 1985 workers on the metro line worst affected took strike action, thereby signalling their refusal to work with this level of violence. They were successful – security measures on the line were improved and the level of violence fell. Since 1985 there have been stoppages in protest against violence on either metro or bus lines almost every year, and these strikes have enjoyed the support of commuters. My point is that violence in any given society meets with a degree of tolerance which enables it to continue or with rejection that will eventually force it to stop.

In Paris a man beating a woman in the street will not cause sufficient public offence for him to be forced to stop unless his violence assumes extreme levels. A severe public hiding of a small child or a dog, however, will cause a major outcry and will not be allowed to continue. In Belfast a man cannot beat up his wife publicly, and a priest could not be attacked in the street, but there has yet to be a strike in protest against threatening letters, which means that the degree of tolerance of this particular form of violence (or threat of violence) is sufficient to permit the formidable efficiency of such letters. No one will even bother to apply for a job if he feels that he will not be safe either at work or on the way to work. Physical violence is in itself discriminatory.

Discrimination is bad, but it is met with a great deal of acceptance or resignation. Some Unionists who have looked at the problem even try to place the blame for discrimination at the door of Catholics themselves. Gregory Campbell, a DUP councillor, wrote a pamphlet in which he claimed that the statistics used by the Fair Employment Agency and various academics overlook a number of factors.[16] Campbell argued that Catholics have a higher birth rate than Protestants so more Catholic school-leavers are seeking too few jobs, even though this argument had been countered a few years before by a researcher who showed that the same differences in employment existed in Belfast in 1901 when the difference between the two communities' fertility rates was negligible.[17] The employment gap between Catholics and Protestants did not narrow between 1901 and 1951, and was in fact bigger than that between blacks and whites in Birmingham in 1975. Campbell also tried to prove that Northern Ireland is entering a process of reverse discrimination because older Protestants employees are gradually being replaced by younger Catholics and it is only a matter of time until the balance of the entire workforce is fundamentally altered.

The Fair Employment Agency

The Fair Employment Agency was established in 1976 to promote equality of opportunity in employment and to eliminate discrimination. The original working party was strongly opposed to quotas and chose instead to stress 'affirmative action'.[18] Discrimination was to be made unlawful, but the emphasis was to be placed on negotiation as criminal penalties were assumed to be likely to provoke sectarian sensibilities and thus be counter-productive.

The *Guide to Effective Practice* published by the FEA goes to extraordinary lengths to avoid using the term 'quotas'. Affirmative action is defined as:

Those special measures that an employer can take to promote a more representative distribution of employment in the workforce in the event of the existing representation of either the Protestant or Roman Catholic community being less than might reasonably be expected.

Recruitment should operate on the merit principle and discrimination is illegal, but reverse discrimination, the reserving of a set proportion of jobs for Catholics, would be a quota system and so is illegal. It is also illegal to favour certain groups or individuals to help correct a historical imbalance in employment.

What, then, does 'good practice' really mean? Employers are supposed to monitor their workforce, in other words record the 'perceived religious affiliation' of employees. The FEA suggests the ending of word-of-mouth recruitment and replacing it with the advertising of all vacancies in ways which will reach all potential candidates. Employers should increase the awareness of pupils of any under-represented minority and preferential treatment of ex-members of the security forces should end. Management should set goals and timetables for a redress of any imbalance. This is sometimes understood as being tantamount to a quota system, but this would be incompatible with the merit system and so illegal. Religion may not be taken into account in the recruitment process. All selection must be – and must be seen to be – on the merit principle.

Advice is also given to the trade unions, which are supposed to co-operate with employers in fighting discrimination. Unions must not themselves discriminate by treating certain members less favourably than others, and are supposed to treat as offences acts of discrimination like intimidation and unfair dismissal by their members. It is worth noting that the FEA is much tougher with the unions than it is with employers: it asks them to expel any member found guilty of discrimination, but its demands are much milder when addressing employers.

The FEA guidelines for effective practice, although meant to promote 'affirmative action', are mostly negative – 'Stop doing this, don't do that' – and the agency has had only limited success. There are very few complaints, and most of them are not followed through. Discrimination is very difficult to prove in court, the main reason being that it is such a 'natural' or 'traditional' way of doing things in Belfast. Informal recruitment practices are a major factor, and the way skilled craft unions have long sought to control recruitment and apprenticeships in Britain and elsewhere has in Belfast acquired sectarian overtones. The FEA has, however, had some success in the public sector, higher grade non-manual occupations and larger firms in the private sector.

The relative failure of the FEA has given rise to considerable criticism, and the SDLP claims that the only significant improvement is to be found in the public sector, but mostly in lower grades and middle management. The main incentive for signing the FEA's register has been the government's announcement that this is compulsory for companies tendering for government contracts. Only 24 firms had signed before this announcement in 1981, but within six months this number had increased to 497, and by 1984 no fewer than 6,335 companies had signed. Not a single employer has been removed from the register for job discrimination. The SDLP still holds the same basic position as the FEA and calls for 'targets' not quotas.[19]

Despite all the precautions it has taken, the FEA is criticised by Unionists who claim that it operates reverse discrimination and that counting heads in the workplace creates social tension because it is discriminatory. The very failure of the Agency is also used against it – if between 1976 and 1979 there were only eight proven cases this only goes to show that job discrimination does not really exist in Northern Ireland and there is therefore no need for the FEA.

The MacBride Principles created such an uproar that one might have thought that they would be very different from those of the FEA, but they are not.[20] Their aim is to 'increase the representation of the under-represented religious group' and the protection of minority employees. This is to be achieved by active recruitment of minority employees and public advertising of all jobs. The principles are the same as those of the FEA, and there is even the same note of caution – efforts to increase minority recruitment 'should not be construed to imply a diminution of opportunity for other applicants'. This, however, is not a matter of quotas or reverse discrimination. Peter Archer, Labour's front-bench spokesperson on Northern Ireland when the MacBride Principles were launched, said in supporting the MacBride Principles that he distinguished between affirmative action and the imposition of quotas. Affirmative action, he claimed, is possible without resorting to reverse discrimination which would simply increase tension and prove counter-productive.

Though the MacBride Principles have been presented as 'reverse discrimination' it has yet to be convincingly demonstrated that they differ fundamentally from those of the FEA. The strongest criticism affects a side issue – the MacBride Principles' insistence that the employer must ensure that applicants are not deterred from seeking employment because of fears for their personal safety.

If there is such a battery of precautions and negative clauses in both the FEA and the MacBride Principles could this simply be because both are what they are desperately assumed not to be – reverse discrimination? In times of lay-offs, closures and shrinking employment they are necessarily so. The change from word-of-mouth recruitment to public advertising is reverse discrimination if jobs are scarce. As in Britain, redundancies are operated on the principle of 'last in, first out', which can only result in discrimination if most employees with long service are disproportionately from one religious group. Does this mean that management should sack older Protestant employees and keep on their younger Catholic counterparts? If so, is this not reverse discrimination? If not, then what does it mean? Affirmative action sounds much more pleasant than reverse discrimination because it means sharing a bigger cake, but the sad reality is that in Belfast the employment cake is shrinking. The FEA says that it is illegal to favour one group in order to correct an historical imbalance in employment, a statement which, if taken literally, would be the agency's death sentence. Why on earth was the FEA founded if not to help correct an historical imbalance in employment?

When there has been long-standing inequality any concrete step to counter it necessarily appears as 'reverse discrimination' to the holders of ancient privileges, however minor these may be in reality. Even research into that inequality is seen as a threat and so becomes a political battlefield.

Belfast is by no means the only place where this debate is taking place, and there are a number of examples of affirmative action in industrialised countries including the United States, Britain and France. As far back as 1967 the Plowden Report in Britain acknowledged that the underprivileged need better schools and a higher pupil-teacher ratio if the cycle of deprivation was to be broken. Various urban programmes in all three countries grant special resources to certain areas. In Britain and France they officially benefit everybody, black and white, immigrant and native, but in effect they benefit the black or immigrant population disproportionately. The tendency in both countries is to present such programmes as the technical application of welfare, job training and housing policy rather than as consciously anti-racist and anti-discriminatory. How is it that the explicit use of quotas to counter disadvantage based on gender and race is found in the USA, the country which is least welfare-minded, while in Britain, and even more in France, politicians are frightened to use the term quotas? Are they afraid of a possible backlash? In France there are always complaints when there is a large slum-clearance project in a predominantly Algerian neighbourhood; the National Front is quick to point out that public money is being spent 'on them'. We have seen that the DUP's response to the FEA and affirmative action is to call it reverse discrimination; the phrase has even crossed over into the political arena, and one loyalist described the Anglo-Irish Agreement to me as 'reverse discrimination gone mad'.

Writing as someone who does not need to maintain his support from any particular sector of the Belfast electorate, it is quite clear to me that the difference between affirmative action and reverse discrimination lies in the result. Quotas are targets that have been reached and reverse discrimination is affirmative action that works. Words and jobs are both part of the battlefield in Belfast.

Notes

1   *Belfast Telegraph*, 3 December 1987.
2   Bob Rowthorn, 'Northern Ireland, An Economy in Crisis' in Paul Teague (ed.), *Beyond the Rhetoric: Politics, the Economy and Social Policy in Northern Ireland*, London 1987, p. 118.
3   *Financial Times*, 19 October 1988.
4   *Belfast Telegraph*, 15 October 1987.
5   Ken Maginnis, *Financial Times*, 19 October 1988.
6   Paddy Devlin, *Yes, We Have No Bananas – Outdoor Relief in Belfast 1920–1939*, Belfast 1981.
7   Winifred Campbell, 'Down the Shankill', *Ulster Folk Life*, Vol. 22, 1976.
8   Robert Harbinson, *Song of Erne*, Belfast 1987, p. 32.
9   Helen Burke, *The People and the Poor Law in Nineteenth Century Ireland*, Littlehampton 1987, p. 193.
10   Poor Law Guardians' minutes, 8 August 1929, quoted in Devlin, op. cit., p. 81.
11   Ibid.
12   Ibid., p. 82.
13   Quoted in ibid., p. 106. .
14   C. McCrudden, 'The Experience of the Legal Enforcement of the Fair Employment (NI) Act 1976' in R.J. Cormack and R.D. Osborne (eds), *Religion and Employment in Northern Ireland*, Belfast 1983; SDLP, 'Equal and Just Opportunities for Employment', document presented to the 16th annual conference, November 1986; R.J. Cormack and R.D. Osborne, 'Inequality of Misery', *New Society*, 22 November 1985; D.J. Smith, *Equality and Inequality in Northern Ireland*, London 1987; Robert Miller, 'Evaluation Research Ulster Style', *Network* (British Sociological Association), October 1988; D.J. Smith, 'No Substance to Criticism', *Fortnight*, December 1988.
15   Robert Miller and Bernadette Hayes, 'The Labour Market Experiences of an Educational Elite', paper given at the International Colloquium on Gender and Class, University of Antwerp, 1989.
16   Gregory Campbell, *Discrimination, the Truth*, Belfast 1987. See also, John Morrisson on the Fair Employment Agency, *Sunday News*, 24 January 1988.

17   A.C. Hepburn, 'Employment and Religion in Belfast 1901–1951' in Cormack and Osborne (eds), op. cit.
18   'Religious Equality of Opportunity in Employment' in *Guide to Effective Practice*, Department of Economic Development, Northern Ireland, September 1987.
19   SDLP, op. cit.
20   The MacBride Principles were signed by the late Sean MacBride, Dr John Robb (a Northern Ireland Protestant and Senator in the Republic), Inez McCormack (a NUPE official in Belfast) and Father Brian Brady (a Belfast priest). On the discussion, see Michael Farrell, 'The MacBride Principles', *Listener*, 24 September 1987, and Peter Archer MP and Stuart Bell MP, 'Labour Party Statement on Discrimination', July 1986.

3 The People's War

Riots and Communities

In 1801 two masons struck work, or, as the expression then was, they 'conspired to raise the wages', and were punished with three months' imprisonment.[1] In 1802 six Belfast shoemakers were jailed for entering into an illegal combination. In 1803, apparently, combination assumed almost epidemic proportions and an official notice warned:

> Many unlawful combinations now exist among the different workmen, artificers and manufacturers of the town ... by which an attempt is made to regulate according to their pleasure the price of wages.[2]

In the first half of the nineteenth century Belfast's skilled workforce was masculine, Protestant and trying to organise. The iron moulders' union was founded in 1826, the boilermakers' in 1841 and the Amalgamated Society of Engineers in 1851. These men were also known for their intense sectarianism; they organised Orange Lodges in the workplace and mixed into a unique obsession the defence of their jobs and a deeply entrenched anti-Catholicism. This religious sectarianism corresponded with their daily experience; in the textile industry, for example, the jobs of supervision and the maintenance of machinery were held by skilled Protestant men surrounded by thousands of poorly paid Catholic women. As far as their work was concerned, those men experienced the Siege of Londonderry every day at the mill.

The typical Protestant man was skilled and as well paid as he would have been in mainland Britain for doing the same job. But the absolute majority of the city's unskilled labourers were Protestants, and they were even more violently sectarian than their skilled counterparts. Active trade unionists with socialist beliefs tended to be older, skilled men, while court records show that the 'ringleaders' in riots were younger and less skilled men. Sectarian rioting, therefore, cannot be explained away as privileged workers defending their jobs. Just as important was – and still is – the defence of a way of life and a community of relatives and neighbours, streets and homes.

It is tempting to try to link the sectarian riots which sporadically shook Belfast with the economic crises which hit the city, especially on those occasions when the defence of jobs became a major concern. Unfortunately, however, Belfast's history does not conform to such a neat pattern. The 1857 riots preceded the depression at the end of the decade, and the 1864 rioting took place when the Belfast linen industry was in the middle of its 1862-67 boom. In 1864 new docks were being built; Catholic navvies were down digging out the mud while the skilled Protestant labour was up above, quite literally looking down on them and insulting them. The tension increased until the Protestants eventually encircled the navvies and drove them off across the estuary. The carpenters – Protestants, of course – struck work to demand the laying off of Catholic labour.[3] Edward Harland reacted swiftly, putting up notices stating that if any Catholic workman was victimised he would immediately close down the entire site, but there was little he could do to prevent the rioting from spreading into the streets and to stop Catholics who lived in Protestant areas being expelled from their homes. It is not sufficient to claim that industrialists never played the sectarian card to divide their workers, but some of them at least did not approve of the resulting disturbances.

The mechanics of rioting in Belfast are often oversimplified by those who see inter-communal conflict as the result of manipulation for self-interested political motives. The example of Edward Harland in 1864 is not meant as a vindication of a particular individual, or of industrialists as a group, but simply to try better to understand how sectarian rioting actually functioned in Belfast at the time. If anybody insists on posing the unanswerable question – who was 'to blame' for sectarian conflict in Belfast? – Harland's reaction at least tells us who was not to blame on a specific occasion. The shipyard owners thought that they were in charge of whatever happened on their premises and their intervention was quick and effective: rioting within the yard ceased immediately. A few years later in the same shipyards discrimination and victimisation were all too often condoned, if not encouraged, by the employers.

This was the case in the 1890s when the question of Home Rule came to dominate the political scene. After the defeat of the Home Rule Bill at Westminster there was widespread rioting in Belfast, both in the streets and in the shipyards. The difference in Harland and Wolff's reaction in 1864 and 1893 is striking. The company felt threatened by Home Rule, not surprisingly as it depended entirely on orders from the mainland to stay in business. 'Moreover,' as the firm's historians note, 'they had a duty to their workforce,' many of whom had come over from British yards to work in Belfast.[4] The management established secret plans for withdrawal to Britain, primarily to Liverpool, in the eventuality of the Home Rule Bill being passed. During the 1892 election campaign 190 of Harland and Wolff's 225 Catholic employees (who represented less than 10 per cent of the workforce) were forced out of the yard. On this occasion, unlike in 1864, the owners did not respond, as they wished to keep their predominantly Protestant workforce. Skilled labour was looking across the Irish Sea and the employers, fearful of a head-on clash with their workforce, kept silent.

As the struggle for Home Rule intensified from 1880 onwards divisions between loyalists and nationalists became deeper and more bitter. The Boer War was seized upon as an opportunity for each side to show where it stood. In Catholic neighbourhoods bonfires were lit to celebrate British defeats, while the capture of Pretoria by British troops was the occasion for Protestant workers to march through the streets singing patriotic songs.

The most violent riots were those of 1920 at the time of the war that led to the independence of the Free State. A contemporary witness, G.B. Kenna, is interesting as an exponent of the conspiratorial view of rioting. For Kenna, rioting and pogroms were the result of an Orange Order plot fomented with the help of industrialists worried by strikes and social tension. In a manuscript of some 200 pages Kenna does not once mention that there was a war raging between Britain and nationalist Ireland at the time, and that in this war the majority of Belfast's population felt itself to be on the frontline of the British cause. Kenna's view was a simplistic one: he believed that, shaken by the 1919 strikes for a 40-hour week in the shipyards, Belfast's employers were afraid of losing their control over the workers and so played the sectarian card as the best way of restoring their authority. So, when the strike was over mysterious underground leaders, 'the wire-pullers in high places', wanted to make sure that such a situation would not repeat itself.[5] 'They' created a fake union, an allusion to the Ulster Unionist Labour Association, even though the UULA had its origins in the pre-war period, as we shall see in Chapter 6.

On 12 July 1920 Carson issued his famous call: 'You must protect yourselves,' and on 21 July the Orangemen of the shipyards were called to a demonstration. According to Kenna, 'The meeting was a huge one, composed mainly of well paid stay-at-homes who had had the times of their lives during the great war.' After the meeting hooligans began to harass Catholic workers and those Protestants 'who refused to bow the knee to Carson'. The fighting then spread to the traditional locations of the Shankill and the Falls; three Catholics were killed and Catholic-owned shops were looted. According to Kenna most of the men expelled from the shipyards were honest working men whom he distinguished from the 'well paid stay-at-homes'. Loyalist workers saw things rather differently, of course, and justified their anger by the fact that during the war Protestants had rushed to the colours and their jobs had been taken over by 'Sinn Fein shirkers' who were then swept from the yards during the riots.

In July 1920 Protestants 'in sympathy with the red flag of revolution' were driven out of the shipyards as well as Catholics.[6] The leaders of the Ulster Unionist Council encouraged these expulsions and the management, not surprisingly, did not oppose them. In spite of strong pressure from the national, i.e. British, leadership, Belfast trade union branches refused to call for the reinstatement of the expelled workers.

Belfast is part of the Clyde-Mersey-Lagan triangle, and its sectarian riots have much in common with similar disturbances in Liverpool and Glasgow. Skilled workers watched with dismay the inflow of unskilled labourers, 'immigrants' who happened to live in the same country. These inter-communal tensions based on the religious divide gradually disappeared elsewhere in the United Kingdom, only to be replaced by others. They remained in place in Belfast where the national question survived, trapped in the partitioned province, and continued to transcend all other conflicts.

Industrialisation produced stresses and strains in Belfast's social and political life, as it did elsewhere. As we have seen, Belfast was a Protestant town ever since its foundation, but in the early nineteenth century Catholics flocked in and by 1851 one-third of the population of the western part of the town was Roman Catholic.

This rapid change in denominational balance startled Belfast Protestants; in the past they had been noted for their tolerant outlook ... It was almost killed by the spectacle of a strong and compact minority in the town itself.[7]

This minority, moreover, had learned from Daniel O'Connell the enormous power it could wield if it organised itself properly. Tolerance gave way to suspicion and conflict, especially among unskilled Protestants who were in direct competition with Catholics for jobs, and for some historians it was this competition more than anything else which provoked sectarian rioting. Street-fighting was always condemned as loutish behaviour by middle- and upper-class Protestants who were nevertheless determined to keep control of the city and so had to accept and sometimes make use of it.

Riots came to be a regular feature of Belfast life in the 1830s, and became much more violent in the 1850s when house-wrecking and shootings were common. Families living in religiously mixed areas moved out and each community clustered in its own areas where it could feel safe.

Most observers tend to look upon sectarian rioting in nineteenth-century Belfast as if it was the forerunner of the present troubles, but matters are not that simple. Rioting was a common feature in many towns in late eighteenth- and early nineteenth-century Britain, often, but not always, setting the same opponents, Catholics and Protestants, against one another. In the 1780 Gordon Riots in London, for example, the homes of wealthy Catholic families were attacked by 'the mob', while in Bristol in 1831 the Anglican Church appeared to be the object of the crowd's anger. Liverpool and Glasgow, of course, had large Irish populations and saw inter-communal rioting of a kind commonly associated with Belfast. In many industrialising cities in Britain newcomers from rural areas clashed with the older inhabitants who defended their territory and privileges against intruders who, being poorer, were ready to take a job at almost any wage and so posed an obvious threat to the established workforce. This clash has been thoroughly documented, and the history of the labour movement in Britain is full of conflict between unskilled labourers and craft unions. The difference was that in the case of Belfast the newcomers were the oldest inhabitants of Ireland while the established inhabitants of the town were descended from those who had arrived in the island only a century or so previously. Belfast was therefore very much an 'ordinary' city at the time of the industrial revoution, bedevilled by the same tensions and scourges as any city on the British mainland.

Like other cities Belfast was also hit by epidemics, and at the time disease was generally attributed to 'foreign influences'. Although the word Catholic rarely appears in the numerous reports on poverty and disease in Belfast, it is not difficult to read the religious label between the lines. The majority of Belfast's poor were Catholics, some of them Irish who had been living in Britain and were repatriated to Ireland following the draconian 1834 Poor Law. Belfast's port saw a lot of these 'foreigners' camped out on the quayside waiting for charitable help, and the typhus epidemic that swept through the city in 1847 was attributed to a shipload of Irish from Liverpool waiting for a passage to North America and delayed by contrary winds.

In August 1847 Queen Victoria visited Belfast, neatly timing her visit between the typhoid epidemic and an outbreak of cholera which swept through the town later that year. As in any other British city, these epidemics were followed by swarms of reports and enquiries into the reasons for poor health, which exposed the lack of hygiene and proved that the absence of a proper sewage system was a major cause of disease.

The most famous of the Belfast reports took the form of a series of articles in the *Northern Whig* by the Reverend Hanlon, later published as a book, *Walks Among the Poor of Belfast*. For Hanlon, there was a direct link between poverty, disease and lack of moral virtue, and the slums of Belfast provided 'a rank and fertile seed plot of every imaginable vice and crime'.[8] Vice and drunkenness were seen as directly linked, and there was 'a close affinity between intemperance and the grosser forms of sensuality'. In North Queen Street Hanlon counted no fewer than 22 pubs, 'mostly spirit stores and brothels'. The poor are described as savages, women or Catholics – the terms are used interchangeably, and Hanlon had an obvious fascination with the sexual mores of the Catholic poor. Once again, however, it must be pointed out that Belfast was by no means unique in this respect and that moralistic reports in almost identical language were published about the poor in every large industrial town in Britain at the time.

Craft unions throughout the British Isles were founded on the skill of their members, their privileges dearly fought and paid for, and dedicated to the defence of their members against the lesser skilled, whether women, Catholics or, more recently, blacks. The first woman to be employed in a Belfast shipyard got her job in 1963, and it is quite clear that in the job market Catholic men were better treated than women of either religion. This point cannot be stressed too strongly: the tension between the two religous communities is not the result of a plot to 'divide the working class'; the Belfast working class has always been divided along lines of skill, gender and religion, and it is not sensible to try to establish a pecking order of these different grounds for exclusion or oppression.

Economic differentials are nevertheless so clearly intertwined with the national question that it is tempting to believe that solving economic problems will spirit away sectarianism. There is a school of pious good intention which believes that if you take the working-class neighbourhoods of West, East and North Belfast and put them all down in polite middle-class South Belfast you will get a million well-behaved people mowing their lawns and clipping their hedges. A guide to Belfast published in 1902 wrote that:

> friction sometimes does arise between sections of the rougher elements, as in other places. Let us charitably suppose that this may be only an indication of super-abundant energy, which, with the spread of education and refinement, will by and by tone down into mutual esteem and good-will.[9]

In the 1960s Prime Minister O'Neill believed that if Catholics were better fed, better housed and better educated they would cease behaving like savages and would begin to act like civilised people, that is to say like good Protestants.

The mirror image of this view is that which holds that sectarianism is the basic reason for poverty and unemployment. Hanlon bemoaned

> that deep deadly curse of our country – the spirit of party ... Oh! my country! when wilt thou learn to feel that only shame and ruin can spring from thy intestine broils ... such is the wretched practice which has been pursued for centuries on this unfortunate island, and which has made Ireland a hissing and a scorn to the whole civilized world. Is this to last for ever?[10]

Hanlon argued that if a fraction of the energy then devoted to theological warfare were devoted to the fight against poverty 'we should be better men and better Christians', a complaint which can still be heard today in Belfast. Hanlon visited Sandy Row; he had been told that the district was a violent one but his fears evaporated in the peaceful atmosphere he found there: 'I thought it just possible that we might fare ill among men of blood, but in fact, people were tranquil.'[11] He wondered whether the prevailing calm was not due to the influence of the local school where 80 children studied the scriptures.

The different parts of Belfast, although denominationally defined, looked very much like a British

industrial city with rows of artisans' houses and, as
Emryn Jones points out, Belfast's housing standards
were 'comparatively decent' because, as a relative
late-comer to industrialisation, Belfast was spared
back-to-back tenements, and small back-yards had to be
left behind each house.

Early twentieth-century Belfast was a self-contained
city. People lived in very precisely defined neighbourhoods, and often walked to and from work. Many of the
city's inhabitants never went beyond Cave Hill, and for
numerous adults and children evacuation during the
Second World War was their first encounter with
farmland.

Ghetto Life

How does one explain Belfast and its close-knit
communities to outsiders? I once took a friend from
South Belfast to visit another friend in Springfields, up
the Falls Road. My friend from the Malone Road had
never been to Springfields, even though his ancestors
lived in Belfast when mine had yet to reach their own
Jewish ghetto in Lublin. But I think I understand
Belfast's problem. I live in Paris, and recently moved to
La Goutte d'Or, the immigrant ghetto of the 18th
arrondissement. Every Parisian has heard of La Goutte
d'Or, just as everyone in Belfast has heard of the Divis
Flats, but how many inhabitants of either city have
actually visited these notorious neighbourhoods?

La Goutte d'Or smells in summer, of urine, rotting food
and poverty; the local dealers sell harder and ever harder
drugs, the police will shoot suspects on sight and old
people are afraid to go out into the streets. Yet I live in
the middle of the neighbourhood and feel safe, safer in
many ways than in more peaceful parts of the city.
Friends do not believe me, even though children play in
the streets and people chat on their doorsteps or the
broken-down pavements. Shops sell fruit and vegetables
that cannot be found anywhere else in Paris, and these

shops are talking-shops as well as buying-and-selling shops. The assistant knows their language, and the smell of the shop is the smell of home. There is a mosque at the end of the street, and from their windows where the washing is drying mothers watch their children playing. Yet, despite what to me is the obvious friendliness of the neighbourhood, my own sister refuses to visit me unless I wait for her at the metro station and promise to see her safely home.

La Goutte d'Or, 'The Golden Drop', is the district described by Zola in *L'Assommoir*, where the poverty-stricken recent arrivals in Paris from the south and centre of the country lived in the nineteenth century. The names of the cafés – Café du Massif Central, Café de Padirac – still recall their presence, although the owners now speak Arabic and the juke-boxes play music that was never heard in the Limousin. Poverty in Paris had an accent then; now it has a colour, a language and a religion, but the deprivation is the same.

During the Algerian War the population of La Goutte d'Or was mostly Arab, and the neighbourhood was safe ground for underground soldiers on the run. Money was collected for the *Front de Libération Nationale* and, like parts of Belfast today, the streets were patrolled by soldiers and policemen carrying rifles and wearing bullet-proof jackets. From time to time a soldier was shot and the area was cordoned off, people were arrested in scores and houses were ransacked. Most Parisians did not look too closely at what went on there. La Goutte d'Or was a ghetto, Paris was elsewhere and there was a war on.

When there is no war a ghetto is the reverse of what outsiders think it is: it is not a dangerous place but, rather, the only place where its inhabitants feel safe. It is a place where, through family and other connections, people can get a job, somewhere to live and help when times are hard. Properly speaking, a ghetto is that part of a city where people are obliged to live because of discriminatory laws, as was the case in Belfast in the eighteenth century and, most infamously, with Jewish ghettoes across Europe. Late twentieth-century Belfast does not, therefore, have ghettoes but communities – homes and safe places where people know each other. In these neighbourhoods there are no strangers and everybody is one of 'our people'. The church is our church. The kids playing down by the post office are our kids. Even petty crime, you can be quite sure, is committed by our own people. If you get a well paid middle-class job you move to South Belfast.

In nineteenth-century Belfast Protestant men coming into the town were turned into boilermakers, joiners, riveters, shipwrights and riggers, and they found housing near the yards in the red-brick terraces of East Belfast. The best way to find a job was through personal contacts, and many people were quite literally born into jobs. A retired shipyard worker's description of his experience of starting work illustrates the importance of family connections: 'An old uncle had a long connection with the yard, he knew the chairman, so it was easy enough to get us started, my brothers, my cousins and me.'[12] Herbie Atkinson's father was a plater's helper, his brother a painter in the same yard, while his grandfather was a blacksmith there, as were all his cousins and uncles. As many as four generations of a single family worked in the same shipyard. The family connection with the yards meant that a man lived with the yard even after work. A young man apprenticed through the good offices of a relative or neighbour could not misbehave at work without the family learning of his misdeeds. Entire lives revolved around the company; social clubs, sports clubs and rambling groups were all company-based. The reverse was also the case: if home and the street were a continuation of work, then the workplace also witnessed activities which in other cities are associated with the home; religion was an integral part of the life of the yards, and George Preston ran a Bible class at Harland and Wolff every lunch hour.[13] Another preacher was smiled on by management as he persuaded his followers to return wood, paint, brass and other items they had stolen from the yard. Ian Paisley, it is worth remembering, started his preaching career in a small chapel for shipyard workers just outside Harland and Wolff's gates.

Even more important than the shipyards in the creation of residential communities were the linen manufacturers. A linen mill required four times as many operators as a cotton mill for the same number of spindles, and the linen barons were the most important developers of working-class housing because of the industry's need for a constant supply of inexpensive female labour, and providing convenient housing was an important way of securing that workforce. Very early starting times, long working hours and low wages combined to force women to live as close as possible to the mill. Both the Falls and the Shankill consisted primarily of small and overcrowded houses, most of which were subdivided and sublet to women working in the linen mills. Babies and small children were looked after by old women and older children, or were sent out to baby-farmers who fed them on tea and whiskey.

Male Belfast

Irish society is, like any other, male-dominated, perhaps more so than most. No one seems to have asked the simple question: why is Ireland the most violent country in Western Europe? What in other countries is metaphorically called the militarisation of politics is literally the case in Northern Ireland. Is there a connection, I wonder, between this militarism and the fact that Irish society is that which in terms of law is the least progressive in Western Europe as far as women are concerned? Both North and South of the border women do not have the right to decide whether they want a child: abortion is illegal. In the name of protection of the family divorce is both illegal and unconstitutional in the Republic. In the name of the harmony of family relations the role of women as mothers and spouses is inscribed in the Republic's constitution as superior to any other form of work. The theory is that the good Catholic children of these unbreakable marriages will grow up to love their neighbours, perhaps even love their enemies, because their mothers never left the home. So how is it that the more the mother is a mother, the shriller the war-like slogans and the more real the militarisation of political life?

What seems indisputable is that if a society permits men to inflict institutional or physical violence on women because they are women, then violence directed at people living in a different social sphere will be more readily accepted and condoned. If women are excluded by law or social practice from different areas of social and political life it becomes easier to exclude people because of the neighbourhood they live in or the school they attended. An important aspect of Northern Ireland's 'Peace Movement', which was created and led by women, was a reaction to that exclusion; thousands of women simply wanted to state that they existed and wanted a say in the running of their province.

The main social organisations in Belfast are male. Churches, Catholic and Protestant alike, are male, the difference being that Ian Paisley has a devoted wife who keeps his home-fire burning, whereas the Catholic bishop has servants devoted to his well-being. The Orange Order is male, and women may only join Ladies' Lodges in which they can prepare social events, and are of course expected to serve tea and home-baked cakes to the Lambeg drummers.

Robert Harbinson's description of one of the most important moments in the life of a young Protestant says a great deal about Belfast's masculine culture:

> At my Lodge enrolment ceremony, I had to stand outside the sacred locked doors of the inner chamber, trembling and waiting in a gloomy passage, then before the whole assembly my name was put forward and approved. The doors opened

and my sponsors emerged to lead me in, keeping position on both sides of me. I was marched through the columns of Loyal Sons. I was now shaking physically and almost incoherent as I swore to keep the Lodge password. When I got home from my enrolment, little Helen wanted to know everything. Until then we had been as thick as inkle-weavers. But now the hocus pocus of secret societies inserted a wedge between us ... I knew the Lodge doings must burn unrelieved in my breast and Helen be content with a slap for presuming to enquire into such things.[14]

It must be remembered that the Orange Order is not simply another political organisation, a party based on voluntary membership; at the beginning of this century no less than 60 per cent of all Protestant men were members, and after 1920 there was very little that could be done in Northern Ireland against the organisation's will. Is there anywhere else in Europe where the dominant party's election candidates are subject to approval by an organisation which does not admit women into its ranks?

Such attitudes run right through society in Belfast; in the shipyards riveters considered themselves the lords of the place and saw their superiority as inseparable from their masculinity. One riveter put it thus:

welding is the ruination of shipbuilding ... In my opinion, out went the craft of shipbuilding when welding came in. It was never a great trade, welding ... You take during the war; we had women welding, you know what I mean.[15]

When the phrase 'job discrimination' is used in the Belfast context it is always associated with religion, but if one were to draw up a hierarchy of privilege, Protestant men would be at the top of the pile, then Catholic men, followed by Protestant women and then, at the very bottom, Catholic women. As we have seen, women tend to be concentrated in 'Catholic', that is to say poorly paid, jobs, while men are in the skilled 'Protestant' jobs. As a group women have major disadvantages in the job market, but this form of discrimination is more or less accepted in Belfast, as it is elsewhere in Ireland.

If secret societies have a long history in Ireland this is perhaps because such organisations are one of the best ways of eliminating women from public life. After all, taking an oath is a man's job, so how can a woman be trusted to keep a secret pledge? It goes without saying that paramilitary groups are secret societies *par excellence*. Could it be that a man with a gun wields more power in his own home than an unarmed man? Who would dare conduct an enquiry into the connections between domestic violence and paramilitary activities?

Belfast's internecine conflict is therefore in many ways a gender conflict as well as a religious one. Protestants see themselves as men, with all the qualities associated with virility, while Catholics are 'women': they are emotional, they have a soul, they are oversexed, they breed like rabbits ... This is very apparent in the imagery of the conflict. Protestant demonstrations are exclusively male: women simply stand on the pavements and cheer their fathers, husbands and sons. Catholic demonstrations, on the other hand, put men (soldiers and policemen) face to face with women, shouting, banging dustbin lids and pointing their accusing fingers. The values celebrated in the struggle between the two communities also have an overlay of gender: Protestant mythology concentrates on the male virtues of strength and victory, whereas the Catholic focuses on the female qualities of sacrifice and suffering.

It is often said that religious sectarianism was most intense among unskilled Protestants because they were in competition with Catholics in the scramble for the worst paid jobs, but the case of highly skilled Protestants driving Catholic navvies across the estuary in 1864 and other incidents contradict this theory. There are, however, no recorded examples of unskilled Protestant women victimising unskilled Catholic women in the linen industry. Could it be that Belfast's sectarian conflict has as much to do with gender as with religion?

The Siege

Every factory closure, every plan for new housing, is seen as a threat to Belfast's tightly-knit communities. In 1967 the council wondered whether, in principle, it was desirable to maintain denominationally defined neighbourhoods or whether redevelopment should be used as a way of ensuring the mixing of Catholics and Protestants. Since then the troubles have solved the problem. Peace walls, of which the most famous is that between the Falls and the Shankill, have been built and keep the two communities apart in the most obvious and dramatic way imaginable.

People used to keep to their own neighbourhoods and rarely if ever met a member of the opposite religion, so it is hardly surprising that on both sides there was considerable ignorance of the other community. Robert Harbinson remembers how as a child he believed that Catholics lived only in certain parts of Belfast, the Free State, Rome and nowhere else, and that:

> All Catholics were under orders, we were told, to burn any scripture they found ... We imagined that newly dead popes were embalmed, and then put on display like human money boxes, and that when they were stuffed so full that not another penny could go in, they were canonized and became saints.[16]

Winifred Campbell 'accepted that they [Catholics] were our natural enemies, out to undermine the State, seize power and murder us in our beds'.[17] At the time of the war of independence there was no radio and few working-class people read newspapers, so information circulated by word of mouth and the most absurd rumours circulated about massacres and murderous plots.

The climax of the Protestant year was of course the twelfth of July, with Union Jacks flying from every house, masses of red, white and blue bunting, triumphal arches and bonfires. The various churches were an important part of the community's identity, and in poor neighbourhoods street services were particularly welcome as people did not have to dress up as they did to enter a church: 'The spiritual need was met by open air meetings where shabby clothes did not matter.'[18]

In fact, the street was part of the home. Because houses were small and families large, people spilled into the street. There was very little traffic, and old people were wrapped up well and brought to sit outdoors. Handicapped children played with others in the street. 'It was almost impossible to keep aloof from the community. Any event, happy or sad, became the business of the street.'[19] This public side to private life has not disappeared from contemporary Belfast, and the wife of a political prisoner in either community will think twice about receiving male visitors – women have been tarred and feathered for less.

In South Belfast the gardens are large, protected from the inquisitive by shrubs, trees and walls. People do not see their neighbours unless they choose to do so and invite them round. Children do not play in the streets but in each others' gardens, again by invitation. In times of conflict control of territory is a vital necessity, and if you live in an area where the children play in the street because there are no gardens the safety of the territory becomes a matter of life and death. The logic is very simple: if in a predominantly loyalist street there is a Catholic household in which it is suspected that the man is a militant republican the safety of children and wives who stay at home during the day is at stake. The function of the community is jeopardised and the suspect family must go. In 1972 in Belfast 71 per cent of Protestant households were in streets that were almost exclusively Protestant, while 66 per cent of Catholics lived in streets that were almost entirely Catholic. Since then the physical separation of the two communities has become even more extreme.

In a city like Belfast which is riven by conflict there are a number of reasons why the two communities live separately. The first and most important of these is that of physical defence, and its corollary, the desire to avoid 'the other side' and be able to feel completely at home, surrounded by friends and neighbours who can be trusted. There is also the more positive reason that segregation helps in maintaining and promoting key social institutions like schools, social clubs and churches. Territorial segregation also provides a solid political base; in the case of constitutional political activity it is the constituency which elects councillors and other representatives, and if the struggle is armed it provides a safe haven for the paramilitary group.[20]

Segregation will never be brought to an end by incentives like reduced rents for those who agree to live in a mixed area. When the conflict is as serious as it is in Belfast no one is going to risk life and limb for the sake of a few pounds off the rent. People live where they feel safe – either in a segregated ghetto if they have no economic choice, or in a quiet residential area if they can afford it.

When the process of avoidance and inclusion becomes this important it spreads throughout the body politic. The majority needs it because it feels threatened by those against whom it discriminates, while the minority needs it because it is the only way of securing some of the advantages which the more powerful keep to themselves. For the last twenty years segregation in Belfast and other towns in Northern Ireland has gone deeper and deeper.

When people go out for a drink in Belfast they either 'stay home' or 'go to town'. Going to town means to the bars in the city centre, like the Crown and the Beaten Docket. The atmosphere in these pubs varies with the clientele, and students gather in two or three pubs around the Wellington Hotel where the music is louder, the conversation slightly shriller and people drink more. There is no sectarian barrier in these pubs and people clearly feel at home. If you live in Ballymurphy, the Ardoyne or Ballymacarrett 'home' means the drinking club down the street where you will hear familiar songs and see familiar faces, and there is a man at the door who will check that only members of 'the family' are allowed in. (The same rule applies in the Common Room at Queen's, by the way, where a membership card or invitation is also needed. There the conversation is more muffled, the music low or non-existent and those whose voices get a bit loud after ten o'clock are probably post-graduates or junior fellows.)

In the Springfields drinking club you also have to be accompanied, and sign your name in the visitors' book. Then you are allowed into the warm atmosphere of a club where everybody knows one another. At the bar a young man is talking to a friend about a hurley match in a public park the previous Sunday. He recounts the story as if he were an army officer after a victorious battle: the territory has been marked by hurling on the sabbath in the same way as hoisting a flag. It is now 'ours' – or 'theirs', depending on where you stand. In Northern Ireland's second city the first decision of the council after the reform of the electoral system gave a majority to the nationalists was to change the city's name from Londonderry to Derry. The town had been conquered and the flag changed. In a culture as attuned as Belfast's to the meaning of political symbols local people do not need these signposts to find their bearings, but they tell outsiders which territory they are on.

An ethnic community is constituted first by a common territory, and a great deal of Belfast's politics is about control of territory. The DUP led the famous Poleglass campaign against the construction of council flats in Lisburn, an overspill from Catholic West Belfast, because it felt that the new homes would be a Catholic intrusion in Protestant territory. The first act of any community is to define the frontiers within which it lives and to ensure its defence against external threats. The supreme punishment, tantamount to the death penalty in ancient cities, was expulsion beyond the city walls.

The modern nation is the result of a common history, territory and culture, and is founded on a political contract which recognises, rightly or wrongly, that above and beyond personal, group and class interests the state represents the most general interests of those who constitute the nation. Individuals and groups relinquish part of their freedom because they consider that the state to which they surrender that part of their freedom is the guarantee of their protection. Without the recognition of this contract there is no politics but only armed conflict, the law of the jungle in which the most powerful rule. Within a nation state there are police forces and courts of law whose authority is accepted, but there is no equivalent in international relations. France was condemned dozens of times in the United Nations during the war in Algeria, but this never prevented her from waging a war against the indigenous population; the war ended when Algerian military power was sufficient to force the French to the conference table. The United States have been condemned on countless occasions by international bodies, but it was on the politico-military field that the war in Vietnam finally came to an end, not in the chamber of the United Nations.

In Ireland during British rule such a contract was impossible, and the majority of the population were to all intents and purposes foreigners in their own land. For the last sixty years in Northern Ireland the situation has been the same for Catholics, who have been seen as aliens in a Protestant state for a Protestant people. The absence of a contract does not mean that politics disappears but that politics becomes a warlike activity. Catholics try to carve out a territory in which they can survive as a community, while Protestants defend territory which they consider to be besieged by an alien community threatening their fundamental values. With a contract the State stands out with a capital S, without a contract the state has adjectives attached: it is Protestant, Catholic, Afrikaaner or whatever, but not the state of all citizens. The police force is, of course, an overwhelmingly Protestant body, and the social services are considered as heavily biased towards one section of

the population, as are housing and health.[21] John Darby
has shown how the marking out and defence of territory
leads 'spontaneously' to the militarisation of politics and
a view of politics in which relations are always those of
victory or defeat, gain or loss of territory.

If there is a fundamental distrust of the police, the
welfare services, the state itself in fact, the natural
response of the group which is discriminated against and
excluded is to organise its own services as far as it can,
just as the Saint Vincent de Paul Society provided
welfare for Catholics in Belfast between the wars.

Once this pattern is firmly established it rolls on and
on and everything becomes grist to the mill. The banks
are said to be biased against Catholics living in certain
districts so nationalists create the Credit Union Bank to
help their own people in getting mortgages. Organising
drinking clubs is not only one obvious way of organising
the community's social life but also an easy way for
various organisations to make money.

But the real crux is the police and the courts of law.
What do you do in the Falls Road when you cannot call
the police? As is well known, joy-riding – stealing a car in
the area in which they live, driving it as fast as they can
into the city-centre and high-tailing it back home if they
are spotted by the police – has been a popular pastime
among young people in Belfast for a number of years.
Who in West Belfast will call in the police? The
community meets and people complain. They want the
kids punished and name names. After all, they had
worked hard to get their car, the hire purchase has not
been paid off, the insurance doesn't cover joy-riding and
now it's a complete write-off. There is a suggestion that
someone who knows how to use a gun might have a few
words with the joy-riders – surely that will stop them.
The word is passed on, but the miscreants are not
intimidated. The organisation which can blow up the
hotel in which the Prime Minister is staying is about to
lose face at home because a few young hooligans are not
afraid of it. The paramilitaries take the kids to a quiet

cellar where they 'try' them and then beat them up; if the offence is repeated they kneecap them. The para-militaries become the sheriffs of Belfast's Wild West. They shoot traitors and tar-and-feather young women who go out with British soldiers. Where in this sort of kangaroo trial are the rules and the rights of the defendant, let alone the opportunity to be represented by a lawyer?

The same sort of thing happens elsewhere. Dublin is the victim of a major hard-drug epidemic and an organisation called Concerned Parents Against Drugs was formed to fight off drug-dealers. Sinn Fein and the IRA issued bold statements: they knew who the big bosses were and would intervene to force those concerned to move out of the area. There was a general rumbling of the voice and flexing of muscles and politics became that little bit more Rambo-ised. In France local politicians, first Communists then the National Front, denounced drug-dealers who, it just so happened, were Arabs, and organised a demonstration of 'angry parents' outside the flats where they lived in order to get a few more votes in the forthcoming elections. The strange Robin Hood-cum-Rambo figure personified by the paramilitary group, which has itself prevented the writ of law extending into the territory it controls, says: 'If the state is powerless then we will take the law into our own hands.' The sort of society which would emerge in Belfast if the men of arms really had their way would be truly terrifying, much worse than that which already exists.

It goes without saying that the police and the authorities more generally frown upon this trend towards self-organisation, but in Belfast it is spreading. In Protestant districts the tendency has always been to use the police to solve this sort of problem – the state was a Protestant state, after all, and so was its police force, but now Stormont is gone, there is direct rule and few people really trust the Northern Ireland Office – and there are signs that this sort of self-organisation is growing in loyalist districts.

The state frowns upon this sort of activity because it is,

by definition, 'subversive', and sometimes the fact that they are considered subversive turns such groups into subversive organisations. Too much harassment can turn good-natured community organisers into rebels.

Before the current round of troubles erupted Belfast was a relatively law-abiding city. Between 1960 and 1964 there was only one murder reported in Belfast, and even today, if terrorist-related crime is excluded, Belfast's record is better than that of most parts of the mainland. A Home Office survey published in 1990 was pleased to report that not only was the incidence of crime much lower in mainland Britain than many Western European countries but also that 'Northern Ireland enjoys the lowest crime rate in Western Europe.'[22] In Britain, according to a not untypical Ulster commentator, there are all the problems associated with racism, vandalism and mindless criminal behaviour because of 'some ill-educated and morality-free lower class youth in Britain's inner cities' and 'the ineptitude and irresponsibility of uncaring parents and the systematic ridiculing of morality and religion'.[23] In Belfast, where morality and religion are taken seriously, there is less 'normal' criminality, which means that people kill each other for really important issues, not for trifles. This is because Belfast, with its closely-knit communities, still retains many of the features of a rural society, and is indeed a good place to be when there is no shooting or bombing.

On 2 December 1987 in the centre of Belfast I heard a group of carol-singers entertaining shoppers with 'Hark the Herald Angels Sing'. Next day George Seawright, a loyalist politician, died in hospital after a two-week death agony. He had been shot in the head by the Irish People's Liberation Organisation, an INLA splinter group. Seawright had become famous in 1984 when he suggested at a meeting of the Belfast Education and Library Board that they should buy an incinerator and burn Catholics and their priests in it. After the mass killing in Enniskillen on Remembrance Day in November 1987 the gala fireworks display after the opening concert of the Queen's Festival was postponed because it was felt that 'It would not be proper to go ahead with the fireworks display tonight.'[24] The fireworks were let off on the final night, two weeks later.

Notes

1   George Benn, *The History of the Town of Belfast*, Belfast 1880, p. 122.
2   Ibid., p. 39.
3   Michael Ross and John Hume, *Shipbuilders to the World, 125 Years of Harland and Wolff*, Belfast 1986, p. 20.
4   Ibid., p. 52.
5   G.B. Kenna, *Facts and Figures of Belfast Pogroms, 1920–1922*, Dublin 1922. 'Kenna' was the pen name of John Hassan, a Catholic priest in the parish of Saint Mary in Belfast in the 1920s, and, although reference is made to a publisher, this book was never printed and remained as a manuscript, which can be consulted in the British Library. Kenna's language is, of course, characteristic of conspiracy theorists the world over, and would repay serious study by anyone with an interest in paranoia.
6   Moss and Hume, op. cit., p. 226.
7   J.C. Beckett in Beckett and Glassock (eds), *Belfast – The Origin and Growth of an Industrial City*, London 1967, pp. 187–8.
8   G. Hanlon, *Walks Among the Poor in Belfast*, Belfast 1853, p. 5.
9   *A Guide to Belfast and the Counties of Down and Antrim*, Belfast 1902, p. 12.
10   Hanlon, op. cit., p. 33.
11   Ibid.
12   Harry Fletcher, interview in David Hammond, *Steelchest, Nail in the Boot and the Barking Dog, The Belfast Shipyard, A Story of the People Told by the People*, Belfast 1986. This book is based on interviews in a television film shown on Channel 4 and RTE.
13   Ibid., p. 17.
14   Robert Harbinson, *An Ulster Childhood*, Belfast 1960, pp. 127–8.
15   Tommy Potton in Hammond, op. cit., p. 88.
16   Harbinson, op. cit., p. 161.
17   Ibid., p. 7.
18   Winifred Campbell, 'Down the Shankill', *Ulster Folk Life*, Vol. 22, 1976, p. 16.
19   Ibid.
20   Fred Boal, 'Ethnic Residential Segregation, Ethnic Mixing and Resource Conflict; A Study in Belfast, Northern Ireland' in C. Peach and V. Robinson and S. Smith (eds), *Ethnic Segregation in Cities*, London 1981, and Fred Boal, 'Belfast, the Physical and Social Dimensions of a Regional City' in Buchanan and Walker (eds), *Province, City and People, Belfast and its Region*, Antrim 1987.
21   John Darby and Arthur Williamson, *Violence and the Social*

Services in Northern Ireland, London 1978. See also John Darby (ed.),
Northern Ireland, The Background to the Conflict, Belfast 1984.
22 *Guardian*, 30 March 1990.
23 John Bach, *Newsletter*, 18 November 1987.
24 *Belfast Telegraph*, 10 November 1987.

4 The Real War

After the Enniskillen bomb John Robb, an Ulster Protestant and a Senator in the Republic, wore a memorial poppy to the Senate and offered it to the chairman who then placed it in his own buttonhole. In the First World War 80,000 Catholic and 50,000 Protestant Irishmen fought for the British crown, while 40,000 Northern Irishmen and 60,000 citizens of the Republic fought against fascism in the British armed forces between 1939 and 1945.[1] Robb's dramatic gesture was meant to remind people that the two world wars are part of the common history of Ireland, North and South, Protestant and Catholic. In Belfast only a small minority of Catholics wear poppies in November, while for Protestants the poppy is as much a sign of loyalism as of remembrance of the dead of two world wars. On 11 November memories are not the same for the two communities.

During the Second World War Eire was neutral, while Northern Ireland, part of the United Kingdom, was at war. In a gesture familiar in Protestant mythology, nationalists in the South were busy stabbing Britain in the back, just as they did in 1916. 'Let's go to Dublin for the night. We might be interned or held to ransom in the German embassy or see a German spy,' wrote a Wren posted in Belfast.[2] De Valera refused to hold talks about possible British use of strategically placed ports on the West coast if Irish reunification was not on the agenda. The Prime Minister of Northern Ireland, Basil Brooke, responded by comparing de Valera to Hitler. Eire's neutrality, of course, helped to underline the commitment of 'the faithful sentinel', as Churchill described Ulster. When the war broke out Craig immediately demanded conscription in Ulster, but wiser counsels prevailed in London and Chamberlain refused. How could conscription possibly be imposed in a province where perhaps one man in three would have fled across the border to avoid it?

The resentment between the two communities was bound to grow in wartime, and half a century later the ill-will has not gone away. Although the Republic has never been a member of NATO it was always clear where its sympathies lay throughout the Cold War, but this cuts no ice with Belfast Protestants. It is almost impossible to have a discussion with loyalists in which, sooner or later, the question of the war does not crop up. 'Their' neutrality is explained by the Pope's sympathy for Hitler. 'They' left their lights on in Dublin in order to guide the German bombers to Belfast. The ill-will dates back to the First World War and the treason of the Easter Rising, and is still there. Why don't 'they' wear the poppy? It just goes to show ... Resentment is all the greater as the Ulstermen who signed up in the Second World War did so on a voluntary basis but were still categorised as 'Irishmen' and so seen as questionable in their loyalty to the crown. Sam McAughtry, who came from the fiercely Protestant dock neighbourhood of Tiger Bay in North Belfast and was secretary of his local Orange Lodge, recalls his commanding officer's suspicion of this potential Fenian in the ranks after an incident at an airfield. As if to confirm that they saw him as indistinguishably Irish, McAughtry's mates called him Paddy: 'It was the first time I'd ever been called such a name.'[3]

The diaries written by G.T. Harris, an Aircraftsman in the RAF, give a fascinating insight into the views of British servicemen posted to Belfast during the war. At one stage Harris and his colleagues were drafted to work as dockers: 'This morning we go to the docks to get the

lorries out of the ship. Hard work ... I consider that we at
3/6 are underpaid and the stevedores at 17/6 are
overpaid.'[4] He noted the general atmosphere in the city:

> Some people are friendly, but deep down ... an animosity
> [was] lying dormant ... Certain streets are out of bounds and
> we are forbidden to carry arms in the city. The IRA needs
> arms and ammunition.[5]

Harris was also struck by the lack of work in the
shipyards and a general air of apathy: 'The skeletons of
three ships in the shipyards have no one working on
them ... I feel annoyed. U Boats are sinking our
merchant ships faster than we can build them, yet here
the yards are idle.'[6] Belfast seemed far away from the
war and Harris felt 'in the fortunate position of being a
spectator'. He wondered 'how long this state of affairs
[would] last. Belfast will make a good target, you can't
miss it – and they don't trouble about black-out much in
Northern Ireland.'[7] A friend of his returning from leave
in London told him that he had spent a lot of time there
in air-raid shelters and was happy to get back to 'Irish
peace' again. Harris recorded two main complaints on the
part of civilians in pubs: the excessive speed of military
vehicles and the fact that Ulster was not getting its fair
share of war industries. 'I, for my part, would like to see
Belfast shook up by a good heavy aerial bombardment.'[8]
His dream came true in April 1941: 'Belfast has had a
heavy air raid and the war which to Ulster is a far away
and distant affair is now brought to their doorstep.'[9]

The general spirit of demoralisation is confirmed by an
official report:

> The exhortation of English politicians to work harder and
> longer have been a positive embarrassment to the Northern
> Ireland government. It is on record that when a batch of 'GO
> TO IT' posters arrived in Ulster, a deputation of employers
> petitioned for their suppression on the ground that they
> would only cause discontent, owing to the absence of
> anything to which a loyal and willing population might go
> to.[10]

The same report stated that Ulster, 'far from becoming an important centre of munitions production, has become a depressed area'. A year after the beginning of the war unemployment in the province was as bad as in 1932, the worst year of the recession, with 72,000 (21.8 per cent of the working population) officially jobless. By 1943 the principal problem was no longer unemployment, but a Finance Ministry memorandum still struck a cautious note:

> It might not be very judicious for the government to boast of Ulster's part in the war at a time when, in official circles, there is a good deal of criticism of what our workers are doing [there were unofficial strikes in engineering, the shipyards and the dockyards, M.G.] and also criticism of the lack of response of our young men in joining the fighting forces.[11]

The Northern Ireland government was of course very keen to appear deeply committed to the defence of democracy and the war against fascism, and commissioned films and pamphlets to state its case. Unfortunately the response to these initiatives only served to reveal the resentment in British circles at what was seen as Ulster's lack of commitment. Stormont's agent in London, Ernest Cooper, tried to sell one such film, *Ulster at War*, but his British partner's answer was not very encouraging. According to the note sent by Cooper to Belfast, 'He did not consider it a good film and ... did not see why in any event so much time should be given to one and a quarter million people – a community about the size of Birmingham.'[12]

Even the official history of Ulster during the Second World War is low-key in its assessment. In the first few months of the war, 'Nothing like total mobilisation was achieved ... The manpower of Northern Ireland was not being effectively absorbed by war production.'[13] The reasons given in the official history are very similar to the feelings voiced by Aircraftsman Harris. Northern Ireland seemed remote from the war, employers were reluctant to commit themselves to war production and the trade unions refused dilution. ('Dilution' was the term given to the wartime employment of unskilled labour in jobs previously the preserve of skilled workers; in Britain dilution tended to mean that women took on jobs traditionally held by men, while in Northern Ireland it had religious overtones and often meant Catholics working in jobs normally held by Protestants, but also involved women doing 'men's jobs'.) Whitehall policy in the allocation of war production made matters worse as priority was given to regions classified as 'special' or 'distressed', but Northern Ireland had not been included in the Special Areas legislation of the 1930s. Ministers of the Northern Ireland government, moreover, found it impossible to consider their hard-working Protestant province as 'distressed' and to go to Whitehall cap in hand asking for special treatment.

But what word other than 'distressed' can be used to describe the city in the novel *The Emperor of Ice-Cream* by Brian Moore? The daily life of a first aid party in an Air Raid Precautions (ARP) unit reveals the despondency of a phoney war in a distressed city. When Gavin, the central character, returns home in his uniform his brother bursts out laughing. Nobody thinks that Hitler is ever going to bomb a remote and unimportant place like Belfast. Even in October 1940, when Liverpool is bombed and the war suddenly draws nearer, the morale of the unit does not change, while among the population at large there is a feeling of satisfaction at being sheltered from the carnage elsewhere they hear about on the radio. The phoney war appears as a metaphor for a phoney life. People are bored, fed up with life in a backwater while momentous events occur elsewhere. Belfast appears as a city full of zombies, moving corpses who are able to ignore the whirlwind by staying where they are. When Gavin finds himself in a side-room in a hospital run by nuns he broods:

Nothing would change. Out there, in the world, governments might be overthrown, capitals occupied, cities destroyed, maps redrawn, but here in Ireland it made no difference ... Even Hitler's victory would not alter this room. Armageddon would bypass Ireland; all would remain still in this land of his forefathers. Ireland free was Ireland dead.[14]

Gavin even considers joining the British army, but when he mentions the idea to his mother she reacts furiously, recalling an uncle who had been killed by the Black and Tans.

The suspicion voiced by the Catholics in Moore's novel of any British uniform, even one which might have been thought to serve the public good, is mirrored by the historical evidence. According to the priest of Saint Patrick's only 22 of his parishioners had joined the ARP and 'were asking for written guarantees' of their safety,[15] and in fact there had been incidents of ARP wardens being attacked near Divis Street. Catholic volunteers were worried for themselves and their families 'because of the fact that their ARP activities may be construed as a method of Imperial service'. A Catholic district warden was anxious that Bishop Mageean

> would be good enough to communicate to the various churches in Belfast that they are simply volunteers in a non-political, non-sectarian organisation whose duties would be to assist the civilian population and if such information might be publicly announced at each Holy Mass on Sunday next.[16]

Another Catholic warden who wrote to the bishop was of the view that the only way to avoid trouble was for Catholic wardens to patrol their own areas because 'the attitude of most wardens is that we are in the ARP because of our own people, and beyond that, we have no interest in the war of England and France'.[17]

The tone of the correspondence between Bishop Mageean and the Northern Ireland government reveals that both sides were keenly aware that they were not fighting the same war. Not surprisingly, the points of conflict were above all symbolic. The bishop had received

a letter from the Home Ministry indicating that
evacuated children would be given ham sandwiches.
What would happen if evacuation took place on a Friday?
The bishop generously granted a dispensation: in these
extraordinary circumstances Catholic children could eat
meat on a Friday ... Lice in children's hair was another
problem. The Ministry of Home Affairs sent a delicately
worded letter to Mageean: 'I'm very sorry to have to say
that a large proportion of the worst cases are from
Catholic girls' schools,' although the official hastened to
add that 'there are some pretty bad cases amongst the
Protestant schools also.'[18]

No wonder that the Catholic church was not keen to
allow its gates and railings to be melted down for
munitions. In response to a request from Stormont
Bishop Mageean replied:

> With regard to the gates of the main entrance to Good
> Shepherd Convent, I have no hesitation in saying that in
> Canon Law the removal of the gates would constitute a
> violation of the Canonical enclosure of the community.[19]

In fact both religious camps saw the war as a threat to
their beliefs and the integrity of their faith. In a city
where Presbyterianism's hold was so great that
children's merry-go-rounds in public parks were pad-
locked on Sundays it is not surprising that there was an
enormous hullabaloo in the Protestant community
provoked by the opening of cinemas on the sabbath for
the entertainment of soldiers stationed in Belfast.

The View From the South

Given the provincialism which had characterised
Belfast's political life since the beginning of the
nineteenth century, most surprising is the way the city
was seen from the South during the war. In the *Bell*, a
magazine published in Dublin and for the fifteen years of
its life probably the most important cultural journal in
Ireland, leading Free State writers complained of the

stultifying influence of neutrality. In early 1943 an editorial noted that:

> One of the greatest omissions in this war is that our newspapers have no foreign correspondents ... This is lowering and undignified. It dwindles us. It means we are not learning by the experience of others.[20]

Sean O'Faolain, the *Bell*'s editor, noted a major difference between manuscripts sent to him from the North and those that came from the Free State. Contributions from the South were in his view parochial and humourless. The North might be a small province but, unlike the South, it was linked through the British Empire to the outside world, and the writing it produced was identifiably twentieth-century.[21] Peadar O'Donnell, the republican socialist who was also one of the century's greatest Irish novelists, was even more vehement. For O'Donnell, Dublin was dead and empty, and the true capital of Ireland was Belfast, whose citizens, unlike those of Dublin, were in contact with the peoples of the world. Belfast was the only city which could speak for the whole country.[22]

How can one reconcile Peadar O'Donnell's view of Belfast as a progressive and enlightened city with that of Brian Moore who saw it as a stagnant backwater? To O'Donnell, a Marxist who had been born and brought up in a country where atheistic ideas were anathema, wartime Belfast could not help but look exciting. It was taking part in the great anti-fascist war and the word democracy was in every speech. The Soviet Union was held in high regard and there were meetings in support of the Red Army at which Unionists and Communists spoke from the same platform. As in Britain, there was a general swing to the left throughout society; even the 1944 annual report of the General Assembly of Presbyterian Churches contained a eulogy for the Soviet Union:

The Russian planned system has achieved remarkable success: it attempts to discover what the needs of the people are. Plans are laid to meet those needs ... The management is responsible to the community not to a group of shareholders.

Friendship with the Soviet Union was widely used to boost the war effort and was used by Labour and Communist leaders as an argument against unofficial strikes, although these were common, as we have seen. All this no doubt played a large part in creating O'Donnell's optimism about the Northern capital as a centre of change. After all, as an opponent of Irish neutrality, he could hardly imagine an exhibition of Irish-Soviet friendship in Dublin, a city which had turned its back on the war.

The wheels of industry often stopped turning in Belfast between 1939 and 1945. Strikes were illegal, but this did not seem to affect trade-union militancy, and although the war caused some women and children to be evacuated the national question did not leave town for the duration of the war, as disputes over dilution made abundantly clear.

On 17 December 1943 the Prime Minister, Basil Brooke, convened a meeting on the sole question of the dilution of labour. William Grant, the Minister of Labour, Admiral Bevan, who was in charge of the Royal Navy programme in the shipyards, Sir Frederick Rebbeck and a Mr Marshall of Harland and Wolff were all present.[23] Admiral Bevan was furious. Shipbuilding targets would never be met because Harland and Wolff needed 550 skilled workers, including plumbers. It was impossible to fill the vacancies if both management and the workforce did not accept dilution, but the unions refused to accept dilution as long as some of their members were unemployed. It just so happened that the unemployed members were citizens of the Republic, so Admiral Bevan suggested that those Southern plumbers be taken on by Harland and Wolff. Impossible, replied Grant, who was willing to accept 'disloyal', imported workers but drew the line at the Northern Ireland government financing their travel. It was clear to Grant that British trade unions were part of a plot to upset the delicate population balance in the North, and were happy to accept dilution in Britain but remembered their Irish members only when dilution was called for in Belfast. Admiral Bevan just wanted the war to be won and didn't give a damn about the population balance in Belfast. Basil Brooke supported his Minister of Labour: there was no way that travel expenses could be paid to foreign labour. In the end a tortuous compromise was reached: the unemployed plumbers would be sent from Eire to work in Britain, and Whitehall would pay their travel expenses. Then, and only then, would dilution be accepted at Harland and Wolff. So ended a meeting which took up the valuable time of the Prime Minister, the Minister of Labour, an admiral and two important members of Harland and Wolff's management team. In December 1943, when the British and Americans were beginning their long and bloody march up Italy and Leningrad was enduring the siege which cost the lives of 750,000 of its citizens, official minds in Belfast were being exercised by a few hundred pounds of travel expenses for Southern plumbers. The war had well and truly arrived in Belfast.

It is obvious from the example of this meeting that the Northern Ireland government was waging two wars at the same time. The first was against fascism and in defence of empire, and the Unionist administration was constantly pressed by Whitehall to produce more ships, planes, munitions and textiles for the war effort. It had to meet London's never-ending demands so as to prove its commitment and loyalism, all the more so as conscription was impossible in the province. The second war was that against local 'disloyal' elements. The government had to look ahead to the time when the world war would be over but the Catholic and nationalist threat would still be with it. In that sense it is obvious that the war against fascism and for democracy threatened the delicate balance of the

'Protestant state for a Protestant people'.

There was therefore a constant tension in Belfast between the demands of the world war and those of the local conflict. For British officers stationed in Northern Ireland the global struggle was the overwhelming, indeed the only, priority and they simply did not understand the local one. When there was a dock strike and the army wanted to unload its own material the Northern Ireland Ministry of Labour preferred to feel its way gingerly through the minefield of industrial relations rather than allow soldiers into the docks and risk a major incident. The official historian explained that:

> a democratic state must be left largely to find its own wartime level ... People could neither be hurried nor easily coerced, least of all in Northern Ireland where the qualities of independence and individualism were exceptionally strong.[24]

The result is that Belfast came out of the war largely unchanged in terms of the long-term balance of political forces in the city. The Unionist government managed to feel its way through the conflicts created by the war in a way that protected its privileged relations with the loyalist working class. In terms of social tensions and industrial strife Belfast was very much a British city, and there was a short-lived swing to the left during and after the war which gave a temporary boost to the Labour and Communist Parties. Jack Beattie, a Protestant, won the predominantly Catholic seat of West Belfast for the Northern Ireland Labour Party at a by-election in February 1943, and in the 1945 Stormont general election Belfast's three Communist candidates polled 12,456 votes. Despite considerable hostility towards the government the majority of the population remained staunchly Unionist and 1945 was not a major turning-point in the history of Belfast and the North as it was in Britain. What the Blitz, Auschwitz, Stalingrad, Dresden and Hiroshima did not achieve, Burntollet did a generation later.

The continuing and overriding importance of the local war is perfectly illustrated by an encounter Sam McAughtry had in a pub after his return from six years' service in the RAF:

The second day at home I was sitting in the Gibraltar bar on York Street, lingering over a pint, when a man who'd missed the war gave me a blank form. 'Fill that in,' he said. I looked at it. It was for the B Special Constabulary. 'That's in case there's a real war,' he said.[25]

Notes

1   John Robb, *Newsletter*, 26 November 1987.
2   Stephanie Batstone, *Wren's Eye View*, unpublished manuscript, Imperial War Museum, 86/61/1.
3   Sam McAughtry, *McAughtry's War*, Belfast 1985, p. 6. See also Robert Fisk, *In Time of War: Ireland, Ulster and the Price of Neutrality, 1939–1945*, London 1985 and Brian Barton, *The Blitz – Belfast in the War Years*, Belfast 1989.
4   G.T. Harris, Diaries, Imperial War Museum, 86/91/1. 28 June 1941.
5   Ibid., 1 July 1940.
6   Ibid., 13 July 1940.
7   Ibid., 31 August 1940.
8   Ibid., 18 October 1940.
9   Ibid., 8 April 1941.
10   *Northern Ireland's Manpower Resources, Report by J.M. Wilson, 17 December 1940*. Public Record Office of Northern Ireland (PRONI), COM 61/440.
11   PRONI FIN/18/23/319.
12   Ernest Cooper to R. Grandsen, secretary to the Cabinet, 23 March 1944, PRONI FIN/18/24/159.
13   John Blake, *Northern Ireland in the Second World War*, Belfast 1956.
14   Brian Moore, *The Emperor of Ice-Cream*, London 1987, pp. 139–40.
15   Correspondence on the ARP in Belfast is to be found in file EP 5/1 of the diocesan archives. I am most grateful to Father O'Hanlon, who gave me access to these archives, and to his staff.
16   Letter from Gorr, a district warden, to Bishop Mageean, 6 September 1939.
17   Letter from Fitzgerald to Bishop Mageean, 1 November 1939.
18   Ministry of Home Affairs to Bishop Mageean, 23 September 1939.

19 Bishop Mageean to Blake Wheelan, Ministry of Finance, 1 September 1943. File EP 1/42.
20 *Bell*, January 1943.
21 Ibid., July 1943.
22 Ibid., August 1942.
23 PRONI COM 61/266.
24 Blake, op. cit., p. 91.
25 McAughtry, op. cit., p. 170.

5 Protestant Dissent

Has radical Protestantism died, drowned in the national question because it chose the wrong side in that never-ending conflict? Few outsiders, and perhaps even fewer locals, appreciate that Northern Ireland is heir to the liveliest legacy of the religious dissent that once dominated politics throughout the British Isles. Belfast Protestantism is still very much stamped with Calvinism: Ulster Protestants are the chosen people who can enjoy the freedom which comes from adherence to the true faith.[1] The cast of mind created by Ulster Protestantism is a strange mixture of elitism and belief in basic democracy, intellectual tolerance and commitment to a fundamentalist crusade against popery. This world-view has almost completely disappeared from mainland Britain, but it is still very much alive in Northern Ireland where the Orange Order toast is taken literally:

> to the pious, glorious and immortal memory of William, Prince of Orange, who came from Holland to save us from Popery, brass money and wooden shoes, and gave us our freedom.

The ringing tones of the Solemn League and Covenant of 1643 still have a bearing on contemporary politics with a denunciation of

> Popery, Prelacy, superstition, heresy, profaneness [and an oath] to preserve and defend the King's majesty, person and authority ... to discover all incindiaries, malignants, or evil

instruments, by hindering the reformation of religion, dividing the king from his people of the kingdoms from another.

This founding text of modern English democracy has within it the essence of many political speeches and conversations in Protestant Belfast today. Catholicism is associated with poverty and backwardness, the South is the home of popery and brass money – just look at the way they come up before Christmas to buy computers and televisions, compare the state of their roads and ours. No wonder they want to get their thieving hands on the North and are ready to use any means to achieve their goal. The IRA is clearly the modern incarnation of these 'incindiaries, malignants or evil instruments'. There is in Protestant Belfast a fascinating mixture of radicalism and bigotry which one sometimes finds in the same person, but more often in a group of people. This composite person seems to say: 'I am a Presbyterian and a free citizen of the United Kingdom – no boss will ever drive me like a slave, and that is why I am a good trade unionist and also a Unionist. By the same token, no priest will ever tell me what to do with my politics or my private life.' On issues like women's rights, peace and the environment, Belfast's Protestant paper, the *Newsletter*, is one of the most radical papers in Ireland, and certainly far more enlightened than its Catholic equivalent, the *Irish News*. This radicalism within the Protestant community is not well known, although it has been well documented by historians.

Radical Bigotry

In the summer of 1867 some 100 people were charged with various criminal offences after one of a number of anti-Catholic riots that year. Most of the accused pleaded guilty and were let off with a fine, but William Johnston, a law graduate of Trinity College, Dublin and the Master of his Orange Lodge, pleaded not guilty but was convicted

and sentenced to one month's imprisonment. The then
dominant Conservative Party refused to lead a campaign
in support of a prisoner it considered to be a hooligan,
and Johnston was instead defended by the Protestant
Working Men's Association which nominated him for
parliament. The banners at his election meetings proudly
proclaimed Johnston 'the working man's friend', and he
was triumphantly elected to represent South Belfast in
November 1868. He was successful in his demand that
Conservative candidates be chosen by the majority of the
enfranchised population, that is to say by working men.
His power-base was the Conservative Working Men's
Association which was founded in 1869 and merged with
the Conservative Party in 1873, and in 1874 the local
party had a democratic structure and its constitution
dictated that it be composed of two-thirds of working
men.[2] As a Member of Parliament William Johnston
championed the rights of both farmers and labourers,
and when he died in 1902 the Belfast Trades Council sent
a message to his family affirming that he was one of the
very few friends the council had in the House of
Commons.

At this time Belfast's Custom House, also known as the
Steps, was a popular place for public preaching, and
Arthur Trew, the leader of the Belfast Protestant
Association who had organised an attack on a Corpus
Christi procession, was imprisoned in 1901 for speeches
he made there which led to sectarian rioting. His place
was taken by T.H. Sloan, a shipyard worker. Sloan had
made himself famous for his long-standing campaign for
the inspection of convents by the Hygiene Commission.
Colonel Saunderson, Grand Master of the Orange Lodge,
had voted at Westminster in favour of exempting
convents from inspection, and Sloan had made a special
point of attending all Colonel Saunderson's public
meetings and asking the same question: why had the
colonel voted for the exemption of convents from hygiene
legislation? Through these untiring efforts he became
renowned as someone who did not compromise with the

principles of religion or of democracy. The Catholic Church should not be a state within the state and Sloan, the humble shipyard worker, was not afraid to stand up to Colonel Saunderson, the aristocrat, and say so. In the minds of many ordinary Belfast Protestants there was no contradiction between the defence of their church and political radicalism, and indeed these were often seen as one and the same because it was the wealthy who were the most prone to conciliation and treachery.

When William Johnston died Sloan was the obvious choice to succeed him at Westminster. Presented by the Protestant Working Men's Association as a democratic candidate, he was to seek election in the name of Belfast's Protestant working men against the 'fur-coat brigade' candidate of the Conservative Association. The Belfast Trades Council refused to endorse Sloan's candidacy, but only after a heated debate, and during his campaign he was nevertheless able to present a number of well known trade unionists on his platform, including John Keown, a plasterer, and Alexander Boyd of the municipal employees' union.

Sloan's campaign contained all the classic ingredients of Protestant populism: attacks on official Unionism for ignoring the interests of its working-class supporters, opposing temperance regulations, being weak in its condemnation of papist ritualism and condoning Colonel Saunderson's laxness. His opponent was Charles W. Dunbar-Buller, who came from a wealthy Belfast trading family. As far as Sloan was concerned, Dunbar-Buller was an enemy of Presbyterianism, temperance and trade unionism – in a word, he was an enemy of Protestant Belfast. At his election meetings Sloan supported demands for pensions and for the right of tenants to become home-owners after having paid rent for a certain number of years.

Battle lines were drawn up. On the one hand, the Belfast Conservative Association and the Grand Lodge of the Orange Order. On the other, 'the people'. Who was to control Protestant Belfast? The stakes were high.

Surrounded by a loyal band of working men, Mr Sloan had nothing to fear ... the other side had come to see that their day of power had gone, and that in the BATTLE FOR FREEDOM the working men were going to win.[3]

The election took place on 18 August 1902. Sloan received 3,795 votes, Dunbar-Buller 2,669. In Sandy Row, which Sloan described as the 'democratic quarter of South Belfast', this victory was celebrated with street demonstrations, bonfires and drums. In his victory speech Sloan said that, 'He was a Protestant, and an Orangeman, and a Conservative ... The working men of Belfast had risen in their might ... No more would the Orangemen be trampled upon by the nationalists.'

Sloan's radicalism was such that he was eventually expelled from the Orange Order and so founded the Independent Orange Order, which is still very much in existence and whose most famous living member is Ian Paisley. The story of this schism is told in *The Iron Heel* by Lindsay Crawford, one of Sloan's closest collaborators, in which he stressed the importance of religious protest while leaving vague his allusions to the wealthy and their tendency to soft-pedal on issues of religious and political principle. Crawford's description of Sloan's maiden speech in the House of Commons nevertheless implies a certain awareness of his political radicalism:

> One could not help thinking, as he stood with his hands in his pockets, in that matter of fact style, that it was more like the manner of a working man discussing a point with a comrade.

More interesting but less well known is that during the great Belfast strike of 1907, which involved both male dockworkers and women in the linen industry, Crawford actively supported the radical Jim Larkin and took part in his public meetings. On 12 July 1907 the official Orange Order refused to allow a collection for the strikers at its parade, but the Independent Orange Order raised £59 for the strikers at its procession. Crawford's column in the liberal *Ulster Guardian* was considered as too radical by the owners, and before the end of the 1907 strike he had received two letters from the owners of the paper, the first ordering him 'to confine all Labour matters to the column "Labour World" and to insert at the top of the column a notice disclaiming any responsibility for what appeared therein', and the second to cease celebrating Wolfe Tone's 1798 rising, which he had praised in the paper as an example of progressive Protestantism.

For nationalist commentators, however, these examples of Protestant radicalism carry very little weight. The issue is very simple: those who are opposed to Irish reunification are reactionary, and although there might be occasional examples of rebellion within the Unionist bloc these are only the exceptions which prove the rule. People like William Johnston of the Protestant Working Men's Association, Sloan and Crawford of the Independent Orange Order, T.W. Russell, the turn-of-the-century independent candidate and supporter of a radical reform of landed property, Tom Henderson, an independent labour Unionist MP for the Shankill at Stormont in the 1930s, W.J. Stewart, who formed the short-lived Progressive Unionist Party in 1938, were all loyalist in politics and Protestant in religion and so are lumped together with the Unionist elite and their very rebellion is labelled reactionary. A classic example of this approach is to be found in one of the relatively few books on Ulster Protestantism written 'from the left':

> Even now [1976] when at last many lower class Protestants have started to question the establishment party, their challenge is not a reaction to the slums and dole queues but a protest against their party's tinkering and methods of the old days. It is an attack from the right.[4]

During the 1984-85 miners' strike the Belfast Trades Council collected money for the strikers and their families. The collectors shouted 'Help the miners' in loyalist and 'Help put Maggie down' in nationalist pubs, and, according to the files, both sections of the community were equally generous in their response. Is this, like every other challenge from the Unionist camp, to be dismissed as 'an attack from the right'?

Politics in Belfast's Protestant working class has been in ferment for some years, and although it is too early to know in which direction this change is leading, one certain way of misunderstanding it is to dismiss it as the 'poor white' syndrome, a Hibernian equivalent of the racism of the poorest members of the privileged ethnic group in the Deep South of the USA or South Africa. While elements of this type of backlash are clearly present, and it is possible to cite loyalist statements which could easily come from the National Front in Britain or France, this type of labelling does not help us to understand the problem and is simply a way of stereotyping people and so closing off further discussion.

Sarah Nelson was one of the first to point out that since the fall of Stormont and the imposition of direct rule on the province there are signs of radicalisation in poorer loyalist districts. As the different 'reforms' of the Northern state were on the whole accepted by the local civil service there was a strong sense of betrayal by the Unionist establishment. There has been a change of thinking about the paternalistic relationship between the Unionist elite and its supporters about housing, jobs and education. In her interviews with Unionist leaders Sarah Nelson was struck by the persistent concern about the radicalism of the Protestant working class: the UDA and the Loyalist Association of Workers (the body at the core of the 1974 strike) were, the Official Unionists claimed, controlled or infiltrated by socialists and communists.[5] This fear is an old one – in 1909 a Unionist spy who attended a North Belfast meeting to select a 'working-class' candidate for the constituency wrote:

Whose fault was it that there were 2,000 socialists in North Belfast? I said it was the Protestant employers' ... and if the

employers would start and weed them out and give employment to the Protestants and Orangemen who are walking the
streets at present, you would have these men to work and
vote for you on the day of election.[6]

The 1974 strike against the Sunningdale agreement was
and still is considered by many in both Ireland and
Britain to be a reactionary fight, a rearguard action
against progressive reforms, but was, in fact, a
thoroughly contradictory event, as can be seen by
reading through the daily *Strike Bulletin of the Workers'
Association* issued by the Ulster Workers' Council
between 15 and 29 May 1974. For a paper coming from
the Unionist camp the *Bulletin* contains not a few
surprises for those who hold a stereotypical view of
loyalism. The *Bulletin* described Northern Ireland as a
reservoir of cheap labour for British industrialists and
noted the similarity between its view and that of the IRA
which described the Protestant state as being controlled
by capitalists who sweat the working class. According to
the UWC the Unionist hierarchy has organised Ulster in
such a way that in Belfast hospitals the doctors and
surgeons are all from outside Ulster and the only local
people are the cleaners, porters and other ancillary staff.
The only members of the Protestant working class to be
found in Belfast's best schools, Methodist College and the
Royal Belfast Academy, work in the kitchens, while at
Queen's University there is only one working-class
Protestant student for every 29 middle-class students.
The other side of the coin of this fiercely felt class
sentiment is the bigotry with which it often goes
hand-in-hand – the *Bulletin* claimed that Catholic
working-class kids are better treated by the province's
educational system than Protestants, and also attacked
the employment of Asian and African doctors in Belfast
hospitals. One cannot fail to be struck by the intensity of
class sentiment in the pages of the UWC's *Bulletin*, and
nor can one ignore its prejudiced and bigoted underbelly:
the 1974 strike, like Unionism itself, was deeply

ambiguous in the message it sent out to the world.

In 1984 Sam Wilson, a leading member of the Democratic Unionist Party, felt it necessary to write an article to counter the widespread view that the DUP was a conservative organisation dominated by the clergy.[8] The result is a well argued and fascinating exposition of the 'democratic tradition' within Ulster Protestantism. Wilson argued that the background and membership of the DUP produce all the ingredients for a progressive movement and that the party brought into public life many people who had no connection with the political establishment:

> Many of the people elected as DUP representatives would never have had a chance of gaining public office without the DUP because they did not have the right accent, did not live in the right area, had gone to the wrong school and did not have hyphenated surnames.

Because the DUP draws much of its support from working-class Protestants, Wilson argued, the problems of social deprivation, poor housing and low pay which they live with have coloured the party's policies. The result is that throughout the 1980s DUP representatives in Westminster opposed Thatcherite economic policy, and on many issues its policies can only be described as radical:

> In housing, the citizens of Belfast, both Catholics and Protestants, have suffered greatly from the neglect of public and private landlords, and high-handed planners, and the old Belfast corporation and the Stormont government, which authorised the flattening of huge working-class areas, resulting in the scattering of communities.

The DUP's stance on a range of social issues – education, social security, benefit reform, privatisation and low pay – are, like that on housing, on the left rather than the right of the political spectrum.

According to Wilson the principal reason for this

radicalism is religious. Evangelical Protestantism is in itself a radical force and it is little wonder that Northern Ireland Presbyterians played an important part in the American Revolution. As we have seen, they were enthusiastic in their espousal of the principles of the French Revolution and played an important part in the Industrial Revolution because, Wilson argued,

> a faith which lays total emphasis on the Bible as the Work of God is bound to manifest itself in radical social concern and action challenging the structures of society which work against the disadvantaged.

Back to the Bible again, always an embarrassing reference point in the modern world. The French historian Jacques Rancière has studied what he calls the 'dreams of the labouring classes', the time they managed to steal from their day's work to write songs, poems, essays and utopias in early nineteenth-century France.[9] He argues that, fundamentally, what these early children of the Industrial Revolution found utterly unbearable was not the hardship and exploitation they encountered at work, but the fact that they were not treated as human beings. He goes on to argue that the traditional view of the left is that workers hold the key to the future because of their collective rather than their individual identity and are suspect if they wish to lead a life other than that of the soldier in the great proletarian army. There are therefore two complementary forms of contempt for the working class: the conservative one holds that if shoemakers meddle with affairs of state then the government will be bad and so will the shoes, while the socialist version argues that workers are part of a great liberation army and that if they meddle in areas which are not properly theirs they will be deflected from their historic mission. The texts studied by Rancière show that the secret of rebellion is not the knowledge of exploitation – the writers are quite aware of this simple fact of life – but the realisation that they are able to be something other than the exploited worker. In

Ireland both nationalists and loyalists are suspect to respectable conservatives and orthodox socialists alike because they tamper with King and Country, Heaven and Hell, moral principles and theology. They do not behave as workers should.

Skill and Syndicalism

Until the beginning of the twentieth century the North-East of Ireland, and particularly Belfast, was the centre of industrialised and consequently of organised labour in Ireland. Through sheer weight of numbers Northern workers and their unions formed the centre of gravity of the Irish labour movement, but from 1908 Southern Ireland began to catch up with the North following the creation of the Irish Transport and General Workers' Union and the rise of Larkinism, the Irish form of syndicalism. Syndicalism was a militant form of trade unionism which concentrated on organising unskilled labour – in Belfast this meant women, especially in the textile industry, and dockworkers – and whose best known feats were the Belfast strike of 1907 and the Dublin strike and lock-out of 1913.

In January 1907 James Larkin of the Liverpool-based National Union of Dock Labourers came to Belfast to organise dockers and, although his efforts were ultimately unsuccessful, Larkinism later came to be seen by many of the city fathers as a plague even worse than the cholera brought to the city by emigrants waiting for their passage to America. Belfast was hardly fertile soil for syndicalist tactics – in 1898 delegates to the Irish Congress of Trades Unions had applauded the Lord Mayor who in his welcoming speech had described the city as an 'elysium for the working classes'.[10] Belfast's lowest paid workers were worse off than their British counterparts and one historian has remarked that 'The contrast between skilled and unskilled rates was truly staggering, a yawning abyss, unequalled anywhere else in the United Kingdom.'[11] Among the worst off unskilled workers in the city were the 3,100 dockers of whom 2,000 were spellsmen, casually employed on a daily basis, and about 1,000 regular dockers, mostly Protestants, who were primarily employed on the cross-channel quays, and were rather better off. Casual labour on the docks was mostly Catholic.

At the end of the nineteenth century Belfast's artisan elite was almost exclusively Protestant, and Catholics (24 per cent of the city's population) were a deprived minority. Only 10 per cent of engineers and 7 per cent of shipwrights were Catholics, while in white-collar occupations 8 per cent of municipal and 13 per cent of commercial clerks were from the minority community. Catholics were over-represented in unskilled groups, comprising 32 per cent of general labourers and 41 per cent of dockers. It must be remembered, though, that the majority of unskilled labourers in Belfast were Protestants.

The tensions between the skilled and unskilled are universal, and it has been argued that Belfast's internecine conflict does not therefore have its roots in religion but in varying levels of skill in different sections of the population. This, of course, is juggling with words rather than engaging with issues. The real problem remains how to separate skill from religion. Protestants felt that they were skilled precisely because they were Protestants and believed that Catholics were unskilled because they were Catholics. When the clash over skill and lack of skill takes the form of gender relations, in other words if the unskilled 'happen' to be women and the skilled men, would anyone seriously suggest that the tensions between the skilled and unskilled arise 'regardless of gender'? It is a characteristic of many skilled men to consider their work as a male activity which is unsuitable for women, and skilled Belfast Protestants considered the possibility of Catholics doing their jobs in much the same way. They felt that Belfast had achieved economic success because it was a Protestant city imbued with qualities of hard work,

self-improvement, industriousness, sobriety and clean-
liness and, as the discussion over Home Rule progressed,
the arguments about sloth, poverty and backwardness in
the South were easily used against the Catholic labour
force in the North. It is impossible to disentangle
national or religious identity from class identity.

Skilled workers were themselves sub-contractors of
unskilled labour, and foremen played an important part
in recruitment, notably in the shipyards where competition for jobs was acute. Skilled men were very con-
scious of their rights and were quite prepared to strike to
defend them; at the same time, however, they saw
themselves as part of an ideal world in which employers
and employees enjoyed harmonious relations, an attitude
perfectly expressed in social occasions connected with the
workplace. William Pirrie of Harland and Wolff was the
guest of honour in summer 1898 at the annual excursion
to the Giant's Causeway of the Loyal Order of Ancient
Shepherds, a benevolent society with many shipyard
members, and it was recorded that he was cheered by the
workers on their return from the outing.[12]

It is not easy to grasp the strange mixture of class
consciousness and tribalism involved in the fight against
Catholic ritualism, but there is no denying that there is a
strong element of class sentiment present in the defence
of traditional Presbyterianism. There are, of course, class
tensions within both the nationalist and loyalist
communities, and Sinn Fein, especially in Belfast, has
managed to draw support from working-class sections of
'our people' in much the same way that extreme loyalism
relies on working-class support. Whatever these opposing groups are fighting for it is certainly not socialism,
but who is to decide that this militancy is not an
expression of class consciousness?

The generally accepted view of the Irish labour
movement is that it is strong and well organised – over
half of all wage-earners are members of a union,
compared with only about 15 per cent in France and 25
per cent in Spain – but an exception to most European

countries in so far as it has proved incapable of creating an independent political force. In the South the small Labour Party has only been in government as a junior partner in coalitions led by one of the major political parties, Fine Gael or Fianna Fail, while the parties to its left have been unable to make any significant impact, although the Workers' Party has polled increasingly well in recent years, especially in Dublin. In the North the situation is no better, despite early and widespread industrialisation: Catholic workers vote for nationalist parties and Protestants workers for loyalist parties.

The mechanism of this state of affairs is complex, but the overall explanation is quite simple. Ireland was a conquered society and the national question engulfed all others. Nothing seemed more urgent than the campaign first for Home Rule and then for independence. In Dublin during the 1840s the largest working-class demonstrations were Daniel O'Connell's mass meetings while in London they were in support of Chartism. The lament has never stopped: how could Irish workers support a leader so reactionary that James Connolly described him in 'A Chapter of Horrors' in his *Labour and Irish History*? Although O'Connell was not as reactionary as Connolly claimed, he was nevertheless responsible for the reduction of the number of voters in Ireland, voted against industrial legislation at Westminster and boasted that he had prevented Ireland from being infected by Chartist ideas. In the North, on the other hand, the largest working-class demonstrations were those addressed by Carson in opposition to Home Rule and the largest and most successful strike was that against the Sunningdale agreement in 1974. In nineteenth-century Europe socialism was the idea which turned scattered forms of revolt and rebellion into a coherent strategy. Without the hope of a different, better world, downtrodden labourers found it hard to overcome feelings of frustration, humiliation and despair due to their working and housing conditions. In Europe this hope bore the name of socialism, except in Ireland, its Land's End, where the hope that stirred the committed was that of a free country in the South and the protection of a free province in the North. One result of this state of affairs is that the labour movement in Ireland has consistently been judged against criteria that were foreign to it. Nationalists have assessed the labour movement in terms of its support (or lack thereof) for the nationalist cause, while British socialists have tended to consider Irish nationalism as militancy wasted cn a cause not directly linked to that of labour. British socialist leaders have long tended to consider their Irish brothers and sisters as stray sheep in the same way that Southerners considered loyalist labour in Belfast as fighting for a cause that was not theirs.

One point which must be stressed is that although Ireland has its local peculiarities the labour movement has everywhere adapted itself to the national culture and had to come to terms with the local political system. Indeed, the established order's first reaction to socialist ideas has always been to label them an alien import. In France socialism was a 'German invention', in Ireland 'an English invention', while in the United States it was simply declared to be 'unAmerican'. Wherever socialism has achieved major political influence there has been a national price to pay. In Britain and France the labour movement accepted colonial policy, albeit with occasional reluctance, and in the case of military confrontation it has always chosen the national cause. The First World War is only the best known example of the seemingly unchanging law that nation is put before class in times of crisis. When reading about the labour movement in Ireland, however, one all too often gets the impression of reading history as the author thinks it should have happened rather than how it actually unfolded.

In the classic history of the English working class the author provides an admirably clear summary of how social classes are actually formed:

Class happens when some men, as a result of common

experiences (inherited or shared) feel and articulate the identity of their interests as between themselves, and as against other men whose interests are different from (and usually opposed to) theirs.[13]

Given, then, that a sense of shared interests can only develop within a common cultural background it is, for better or worse, clear that this common ground does not exist for Catholic and Protestant working people in Ireland. In the circumstances it is not therefore surprising that radicalism expresses itself quite differently in each camp. What is rarely acknowledged is that there is a bona fide radicalism within the Protestant camp. Perhaps because it has clothed itself in the language of the seventeenth century and based itself on Calvinist theology rather than using the traditional language of the labour movement, this radicalism in Belfast's Protestant working class has camouflaged itself very effectively and become Ulster's best kept secret.

Notes

1   Terence Brown, *The Whole Protestant Community. The Making of a Historical Myth*, Derry 1985; Marianne Elliott, *Watchmen in Sion: The Protestant Idea of Liberty*, Derry 1985.

2   Peter Gibbon, *The Origins of Ulster Unionism. The Formation of Popular Protestant Politics and Ideology in Nineteenth Century Ireland*, Manchester 1975; J.W. Boyle, 'The Belfast Protestant Association and the Independent Orange Order, 1901–1910', *Irish Historical Studies*, Vol. 13, September 1962; Henry Patterson, *Class Conflict and Sectarianism, The Protestant Working Class and the Belfast Labour Movement, 1868–1920*, Belfast 1980.

3   'Jurist' (Lindsay Crawford), *The Iron Heel or the Fight for Freedom*, Belfast 1903. On the Independent Orange Order, see also Boyle, op. cit. and Austen Morgan, 'The Labour Movement and the Working Class in Belfast, 1905–1923', PhD thesis, Queen's University Belfast, 1978.

4   Geoffrey Bell, *The Protestants of Ulster*, London 1982, p. 11

5   Sarah Nelson, *Ulster's Uncertain Defenders*, Belfast 1984.

6   John Gray, *City in Revolt, James Larkin and the Belfast Dock Strike of 1907*, Belfast 1985, p.238.

7   A full set of the *Bulletin* can be consulted in the Linen Hall Library.

8   Sam Wilson, *Fortnight*, No. 201, February 1984.

9   Jacques Rancière, *La Nuit des Prolétaires, Archives du Rêve Ouvrière*, Paris 1981.

10   Gray, op. cit., p. 3.

11   Ibid., p. 6.

12   Ibid., p. 22.

13   E.P. Thompson, *The Making of the English Working Class*, Harmondsworth 1968, pp.9–10.

6 Unionist Consent

The Unionist View of 'Our Workers'

It is widely assumed, both in Northern Ireland and elsewhere, that Ulster Unionism is a political creature so unique that it can only be explained by reference to the peculiarities of local history, even though in mainland Britain Protestantism has also been used by the Conservative Party in an attempt to forge a lasting link with the working class. This tactic, known as Tory democracy, was designed to secure working-class support for Conservatism through an appeal to a mixture of religion, patriotism and social concern. In the late nineteenth century Tory democracy was above all successful in two cities, Liverpool and Belfast. In both cities the clash between Catholics and Protestants was particularly strong.[1]

Despite Liverpool's importance for Tory democracy, Conservative yearning for an inter-class alliance always turned to Belfast when looking for the best example of what could actually be achieved. The *National Review*, an influential right-wing magazine during the First World War, praised Carson above all for the hold he had over working men in Belfast.[2] At Carson's meetings the audience was mainly working-class, claimed the *National Review*'s enthusiastic correspondent and, although the British might consider these Belfast Protestants to be ignorant bigots, they listened passionately and attentively to the unquestioned leader of Protestant Ulster. Carson promised nothing but toil and hardship, but people attended his meetings because they had an ideal for which they were willing to sacrifice their lives. Carson was the opposite of those politicians who visit factories and farms and, realising that wage-earners are in a majority there, promise to enrich them at the expense of their employers. This southern-born aristocrat who was now the champion of industrial Ulster was not the sort to try to curry favour with his audiences by promising them that which was not rightfully theirs.

> He spoke to them, not of higher wages to be earned through strikes and agitation, nor did he stir up strife between class and class, nor did he please fools by encouraging them to agitate for the decrease of armaments and taxation.

Quite the reverse. He asked them to devote their wages, their time and their energy to their ideals: freedom, national unity and the defence of the British Empire. Thus encouraged, the loyal citizens of Ulster become an unbreakable force:

> The toilers in the shipyards and factories, the labourers on the farms – 'the lower classes' as the odious expression designates those who in truth control the Empire – together with their wealthy employers, and the landowners and merchants, became what they had been taught to be – responsible citizens of a vast Empire.

The British Empire was not an abstract idea for Belfast Protestants at this time. The overwhelming majority of loyalists understood that the prosperity of the industries which dominated the city and provided their wages depended on the existence of a strong British Empire. When Lord Dufferin, Viceroy of India, came back to Belfast following the annexation of Burma, William Pirrie was able to tell an enthusiastic audience that orders had come to Harland and Wolff for ships to cater for the new trade, and in the same way the Boer War was an occasion for celebrating the tonnage of Belfast ships used as troop transports.[3]

Carson never failed to remind his flock that the Empire belonged to them in the same way as their homes, their children, their religion, their fields and their tools. If the Empire belonged to them, they must love it and, if necessary, be willing to die for it:

> So, gradually, the Empire came to rank only second to God in Ulster hearts, and in living for and giving to their Empire these people came to believe they were living for and giving to their God.

Sharing such an ideal transcended all class divisions and created a strong solidarity between members of different social classes:

> masters and men eventually understood that they were necessary the one to the other. They ceased endeavouring to get the better of each other; they became as brothers united in their ideal and the Province prospered.

A country with a population sharing such a strong ideal and willing to make sacrifices for it could be transformed into an earthly paradise, a thriving and virtuous commonwealth. Under the influence of Carson's teaching Ulster was seen as an island of prosperity in a sea of Hibernian poverty. The picture painted in the *National Review* was, to say the least, exaggerated, but it gives a very good idea of the way in which Ulster was seen by Unionists in both Britain and Ulster at the time:

> drunkenness diminished ... Vice lost much of its attractive-ness; street rows became infrequent. Public health improved and the death-rate decreased. Homes became happier and more comfortable ... and Sunday after Sunday, in every little whitewashed, unadorned church, these modern Covenanters stood face to face before Him to whom Empire and freedom belong.

At Carson's meetings Ulster citizens were asked to consider the sorry state of affairs on the other side of the Irish Sea where employers and employees quarrelled over a few shillings. To blame for this sorry situation were politicians who had taught their followers to consider themselves as little better than cattle whose 'owners' (trade union leaders) were on the look-out for the best price in the market-place, and did not act as responsible citizens. In Ulster, when there was a war on, there was no question of strikes in support of selfish and sectional demands. Able-bodied men joined the army and civilians worked harder 'because they are a civilised community ... rough workers though they be, they have learnt the first principles of nobility'.

The idea of workers as cattle selling their labour to the highest bidder takes us to the heart of a long-running debate about the hold of 'reactionary ideas' over large sections of the population. There is on the left a well established tendency to consider 'the workers' as mere economic units, ignoring the fact that they have a country, a sex and a religion, with all the ideas and emotions which inevitably accompany these aspects of their being. This debate has taken place on numerous occasions, initially in effort to understand the attraction of fascism for the mass of the population in Germany and Italy, and more recently to try to come to terms with the popularity of Jean-Marie Le Pen and the French National Front. While it must be emphasised that Ulster Unionism has never been a form of Irish fascism,[4] the way in which Carson and Craig set about organising the Unionist bloc certainly has a relevance to that debate. It is also interesting for the light it sheds on the ideal Ulster dreamed of by the Unionist hierarchy.

The UULA

In October 1920, during a flag-raising ceremony in the copper-finishing shop at Harland and Wolff, Craig declared that he 'occupied a unique position when he considered how seldom a member of Her Majesty's Government had the opportunity of coming right into the very midst of the working classes'.[5] In 1935 the annual reception of the Ulster Unionist Labour Association was deemed to be a great success and Neville Chamberlain, the guest of honour on that occasion, confided to Craig that he 'did not think that outside Ulster such a meeting was possible'.

In the Ulster Unionist Labour Association, an organisation centred almost exclusively on Belfast, there was to be found none of the rebellious spirit of Johnston, Sloan, Crawford and others. The UULA corresponded much more closely to the image widely held outside Ulster of the loyalist worker tied to his employer in a servile bind. It is for this reason that the organisation is worth looking at in some detail.

The UULA's forerunner was created in 1914 when, according to Joseph Cunningham, a prominent trade unionist at Harland and Wolff and member of the Orange Order, many Belfast trade unionists maintained that only local employers were opposed to Home Rule. Not surprisingly, Cunningham did not agree with this line of argument and shared his opposition to it with Thompson Donald, formerly district secretary of the Shipwrights' Union. According to Cunningham, 'They were encouraged to organise the trade unionists into a Loyalist Emergency Committee,' later to become the UULA. Their first task was to organise a meeting of trade unionists in the Ulster Hall on 29 April 1914, with entry on presentation of a union card. The massive hall was packed. 'We were told afterwards that the report of this meeting created a good impression on the workers of Great Britain,' said Joseph Cunningham. The meeting adopted an appeal to British trade unionists, and loyalists greeted it as a 'purely spontaneous demonstration, originating with the workers and conducted solely by them'. When the British Labour Party sent a delegation to Ireland shortly after the First World War the April 1914 meeting was constantly cited as proof of the working-class character of Ulster Unionism.

It does not take much to guess that those who 'encouraged' Cunningham and Donald were the leaders

of the Ulster Unionist Council (UUC), because without
the active support of loyalist workers they had no
political future. Their desire to show that Unionism was
not just the party of landowners and businessmen
remained constant. Even before the First World War had
ended the UULA resumed its fight against Home Rule.
On 30 April 1918 John Andrews, a member of the UUC
who was later to succeed Craig as Prime Minister, asked
loyalist workers to act against lying propaganda: 'Some
action should be taken for the real voice of labour to be
heard.' A delegation of ten trade unionists was chosen to
go on a two-week tour of Great Britain to explain the
Unionist position, and Dawson-Bates, the secretary of
the Ulster Unionist Council, pronounced himself very
satisfied with its performance: 'The deputation of
working men which I sent over to England are doing
extremely good work.' Loyalist workers were also sent
over to Britain to participate in Conservative election
meetings. Others made the trip in the opposite direction
and, welcomed by the loyalist workers of Belfast, 'Most
left for home with changed political views.'

From the outset Carson's and Craig's long-term project
was to ensure that there would be Unionist labour
representation at Westminster. The UULA was seen by
the Unionist leadership as the ideal training ground for
docile labour leaders whose presence would guarantee
that there would be no more attempts at independent
Orangeism of the Sloan-Crawford type. John Andrews'
proposal to a UULA meeting before the 1918 General
Election was adopted unanimously:

1. The undersigned, representing the views of the Unionist
majority of the trade unions in Belfast, ask our Ulster
Unionist Council to nominate Unionist labour candidates for
three consituencies.
2. In all questions affecting the Union, they will vote with
the Ulster Unionist Party, but on all other matters brought
before the House, they are perfectly free to act as they may
... think right and proper.

This resolution was followed by the signatures of 21 trade unionists, the majority of them from the shipyards. On 18 May 1918 Andrews acknowledged the superb work accomplished by the delegation to Britain and announced that the Working Men's Watch Committee would send permanent representatives to the directing bodies of the Ulster Unionist Council. He added that in three of Belfast's eight constituencies – Shankill, Saint Anne and Victoria – the UUC wanted to put up working-class candidates. He recommended that trade unionists take part in local meetings and get themselves known, as it was not sufficient for decisions to be taken at the top and passed down. There was strong resistance from local organisations and several additional meetings of the UUC were needed to persuade constituency bosses to accept these trade union candidates. At one meeting Andrews was asked to define what he meant by a 'labour candidate'. His reply, 'A candidate whose Unionism was undoubted and whose trade unionism was also beyond question,' captures perfectly the UUC's vision of the ideal working-class loyalist.

On 1 November 1918 the UULA threatened to run its own candidates in all Belfast's constituencies if Unionist bosses in Saint Anne continued to reject the UULA candidate there. This threat, which almost amounted to political blackmail, was only possible because the UUC leadership stood firmly behind the UULA. The crucial December 1918 elections were approaching and Craig wanted to have his three working-class Members of Parliament and so announce to British public opinion that the UULA was the only labour organisation in Northern Ireland sufficiently representative of Ulster opinion to have Westminster MPs in its ranks. Samuel McGuffin, Thompson Donald and H.T. Burns were duly returned and Craig's dream fulfilled. In his speech at a victory meeting Craig claimed that, 'He had worked in season and out of season to secure labour representation in Belfast and he was perfectly satisfied now.'

The UULA was never a big organisation. In 1934 a

tribute to Andrews presented it as the body most representative of the loyalist working class, although the account books and membership lists show that it never exceeded 1,000 members. The largest loyalist organisation in the 1930s was, of course, the Orange Order which embraced more than half the Protestant adult male population and was overwhelmingly working-class in its membership. The UULA's list of members between 1933 and 1951 includes an artist, a sacristan, a grocer, an architect and a missionary, but the great majority were shipyard workers. About a third were classified as 'labourers'. Only two members were not trade unionists: Edward Carson, its president, and John Andrews, the chairman.

In spite of a number of attempts, the UULA never expanded outside Belfast, and the prime focus of its activity was three clubs in East, North and South Belfast. Organised on the model of the working men's clubs of the North of England, with billiards, cards, music and dances, the one significant difference between the UULA clubs and their English counterparts was a major factor in their ultimate failure: alcohol was banned. 'Presbyterianism strangled them,' as a former member of the organisation told me. The year was punctuated by outings to Portrush, Bournemouth and London. A literary society organised regular meetings, and the UULA was affiliated to the Workers' Educational Association but cancelled its membership in 1932 as a result of the 'lack of interest' on the part of its members. It would seem that the UULA preferred to run its own affairs and did not overly appreciate outside influence.

The executive committee met regularly, sometimes as often as three or four times a week, but the main activity was the general meeting on the first Saturday of each month. This had a dual function. The first was the education of loyalist workers, and each month a speaker introduced a current political topic or more general theme: How to Own Your Own Home, Reasons for Unemployment, Labour and the Nation, The Connection

with India as it Affects British Labour, On Russia, The
Fallacies of Social Credit. Also included in the
programme were events to which wives and daughters
were invited, social evenings with singers and revue
artists and talks on subjects of general cultural interest.
On the whole, however, the subjects were directly
political.

What is immediately striking in the various accounts
of the UULA's activities is how seriously Unionist
leaders took the association's second function. According
to Cunningham, Carson used the UULA as a platform
from which to make important policy statements, such as
that on the 1920 Ireland Act (which provided for
partition and the creation of the six-county state) and to
test the water of working-class loyalist opinion. John
Andrews, who replaced Craig as the UULA's president,
was rarely absent from these meetings and the talks
were given by Unionism's leading personalities – Carson
on 'The War and His Duties as a Cabinet Minister', John
Andrews on 'The New Economy Bill and Public
Assistance Committees' and 'The Present Powers of Our
Government and the Privileges We Enjoy as a Result of
Them', the Minister for Justice on trade union
legislation, Craig on the political situation, and so on.
Unionist leaders used these meetings to air new ideas
and receive a first reaction to them from the loyalist rank
and file. In return, the UULA's members had an
opportunity to mix with the elite, and a small number of
them were offered the chance to become known and rise
to governmental or other responsibilities.

Despite Andrews' advice to UULA members in 1918,
however, the current of ideas was from the top down,
never in the opposite direction. The UULA never
amounted to an autonomous organisation with its own
programme and policies, and did not make demands of
the Unionist leadership. Its leaders appear as minor
figures in the Unionist establishment, token workers to
be paraded from time to time in order to demonstrate the
popular character of Unionism. Edward Carson was

re-elected president each year, and the 1918 annual general meeting duly passed a vote of thanks

> for his untiring and successful efforts to secure for Ulster a Parliament of her own and to save her from the disaster of being placed under a Dublin Parliament. We trust that he may long remain our leader.

Two years later the executive committtee was still grateful to Carson 'for the great and effective work which he has done to lessen the hardships associated with unemployment'. At a public meeting in 1919 the three speeches by the 'labour' MPs consisted of nothing but unadulterated praise for Carson who, at the same meeting, called for the working class to make sacrifices in the common good.

When demands were made they were of a sectarian character. During the depression, for example, a motion declared that 'it was the duty of the government to find employment ... for our people'. There were too many Catholic grave-diggers in Protestant cemeteries, too many Catholic nurses in the hospitals – so many, indeed, that young Protestant women were reluctant to join the profession. In a refrain that was to be heard on subsequent occasions, there were deemed to be too many Catholics, communists and socialists in different ministerial committees, when the UULA had any number of competent and loyal trade unionists it could recommend. These views should not be seen as an aberration but as in harmony with the objectives of the organisation, which were to reinforce the Unionist cause and to co-operate with loyalist employers in order to obtain preferential employment for Protestants.

Even taking this into account, certain UULA statements were nevertheless amazing when it is remembered that it was a working-class organisation. When in 1930 the British Labour government proposed repealing the anti-strike law passed in 1927 the UULA requested that the statute be left in place. In 1931 the UULA declared that it understood that additional sacrifices would be needed in order to overcome the problems caused by the recession and suggested 'that sacrifices should be imposed in accordance with the power to bear them'. After a move not noticeably in accordance with this principle, the reduction in unemployment benefits which was to spark off the 1932 Outdoor Relief Riots, William Grant, a 'working-class' Unionist MP, declared to Stormont that: 'The government had no other option ... the cut was inevitable.' The same evening the monthly meeting of the UULA heard a talk by Ernest Rea on 'Irish Wit and Humour'.

Perhaps the most extreme example of the UULA's desire to present itself as an organisation of a staunchly anti-socialist nature came in 1963 when it passed a motion asking the Stormont government

> to set up an industrial court whereby the trade union leaders would have to satisfy the court that any strike action taken by their union would not endanger the employment of trade unionists or workers outside their own particular union, or the economy of Northern Ireland

This time the UULA had gone too far, even for the province's rulers; the motion was not even discussed at the Unionist annual conference.

Just occasionally the echo of thunder from the world outside could be heard in the UULA's meetings. After the First World War the association officially supported the movement for a reduction of the working week. But when Jack Beattie wanted to raise the possibility of a strike by municipal sanitary and cleaning workers 'after discussion the matter was dropped'. The issue of the 1919 strikes which paralysed Belfast was raised at the end of a meeting, 'but owing to the lateness of the hour, it was impossible to have a discussion,' even though three members of the UULA's executive were also members of the strike committee. During the Outdoor Relief Riots of 1932 the executive decided that each of its members should go to the Board of Guardians in person to ask for an increase in the relief rate. In 1935, as sectarian rioting

once again shook Belfast, 'a long and interesting
discussion took place on the recent disturbances in the
city, but the meeting closed in peace, love and harmony'.
The history of social conflict in Northern Ireland has to
be sought elsewhere than in the archives of the UULA.

The one genuine example of rebellion in the UULA's
ranks occurred during the Second World War. In 1942 a
general meeting was held with the unusual title of
'Question Night'. Members were invited to ask questions,
and these flooded in. Three main themes emerged: the
weakness of the war effort, requests for discrimination
against Southern workers and the demand for full
employment and improved social benefits in the post-war
period. Why did ministers not pay more visits to factories
to encourage workers in support of the war effort? Why
was propaganda in the workplace so weak and
ineffectual? How many skilled and unskilled workers
had come up to Belfast from Eire? What guarantees were
there that these 'immigrants' were loyal? Why did the
government send 'our workers' to Britain and thus let
Free Staters take over 'our jobs'? What measures were
being taken against IRA activities?

The third theme was directly linked to the first, as the
establishment of a social welfare system in the post-war
period was seen as 'a great incentive for the war effort'.
The questions on this subject were too numerous to be
easily summarised, but their general tone is captured in
the following:

> Why are people in industry who produce all the wealth and
> whose work is dirty so badly paid that they live in houses
> without baths, while people who have clean jobs and live off
> these people get better paid and live in houses with baths?

It should be remembered that this was not a socialist but
a Unionist meeting and government ministers were
present and had to answer this hostile questioning.

Three months later in Stormont the Prime Minister
presented his post-war social policy, replying point by
point to the questions asked at the UULA meeting. If the

war effort obviously remained top priority, 'the ideal of a
full and free life for all' was precisely the goal for which
the war was being fought. After the war the slums were
to be demolished, the school leaving age raised, pensions
and other benefits were to be on the same level as those
in Britain and all houses were to be provided with baths.
A general meeting of the UULA discussed and warmly
endorsed the government's programme.

With the exception of wartime, however, elementary
trade union values were foreign to the UULA. In a letter
to Carson the secretary, William Hungerford, struck a
typical note by denouncing the 'invasion' of rural districts
by Catholic 'farm boys' who could become voters after
only a few days working in a constituency:

> But they have no stake whatever in these counties, not
> owning even a blade of grass. Their power in the ballot box,
> however, is as great individually as the Merchant Prince,
> the Captain of Industry or the hard-working farmer.

Hungerford thus touched on one of Unionism's raw
nerves, the growth of the Catholic population and
electorate, and elsewhere in the letter Hungerford
expressed a deferential loyalty when he remarked that:
'You will be glad to know that the Duke [of Londonderry]
had a grand reception and that everything went off very
well despite that the weather was terrible.' With good
reason John Andrews had written to Carson in 1935
that:

> Our kind friends of the Unionist Labour Association are, as
> you know, unequalled in any other community. The hard
> times that they have gone through, when a large number of
> them have been unemployed for long periods, have never
> shaken them in their loyalty to their principles, the Union
> and the Empire, the party, their leader.

The UULA encountered a major set-back in relation to
one of its founders' central objectives – the struggle
against the Irish Congress of Trade Unions, which was

considered to be in the hands of Southern nationalists, and the effort to establish independent, Ulster-based trade unions. One of the organisation's founder-members, James Turkington, tried unsuccessfully to organise an Ulster Workers' Trade Union in the UULA's early years, and there was an equally fruitless attempt to organise on a six-county basis after the Second World War. Protestant workers were glad to support loyalist organisations, but they stood by their non-sectarian trade unions. To introduce political divisions into the trade union movement would have meant weakening it, and the UULA was not seen as sufficiently powerful for this to be a risk worth taking.

But if loyalist workers could not – or would not – create separate trade unions, why did they not try to take control of the existing unions? They had the numerical strength, but seemed to be lacking in the desire to take them over. From 1918, when the UULA was still only the Working Men's Watch Committee, instructions were regularly issued stipulating that only good and loyal Unionists should be chosen as delegates to the Belfast Trades Council. The organisation's annual report for 1944 declared that

> too many socialists and communists hold key positions in the labour movement. For this state of affairs, the loyal workers are not free from blame. It is their duty that only those in harmony with their views should be elected.

Were there deeper reasons for this failure? The answer is perhaps as much cultural as it is political – loyalism's difficulty or inability to make connections with the outside world – and in this respect the UULA's withdrawal from the Workers' Educational Association is of more than anecdotal significance. Nationalists, on the other hand, were able to make links with the wider world, to find allies and support beyond their own community. They were fighting for national independence, justice and the rights of man – ideals which were comprehensible well beyond the shores of Northern

Ireland. Protestant workers were capable of making connections with the wider world, but only if they ascribed to an internationalist, that is to say socialist, creed. Leaders like William Walker, Harry Midgley and Jack Beattie could gain a hearing beyond their own community but, generally speaking, loyalists have only ever felt secure within the frontiers of the North, with friends who understand them.

This insularity was perfectly expressed by Daniel McNabb of Ballymoney, who

> watched with a good deal of anxiety the progress that the Transport and General Workers' Union [was] making around North Antrim ... the minds of the younger generation will be contaminated with 'red stuff' – because in these branches of the workers' union, as they are a mixture of different religious convictions, neither Protestantism or Unionism is ever considered.

The result was that in real emergencies, such as prolonged strikes, the UULA was never considered by the Unionist government to be sufficiently representative that it could be used as an intermediary, and at such moments it was necessary to negotiate directly with the unions themselves. In 1919, when 40,000 shipyard and engineering workers struck for a 40-hour week, the Orange Order rather than the UULA was used as an intermediary with the unions. The Orange Order received a delegation of striking workers and subsequently published a manifesto which noted that the situation 'has been engineered by parties who have taken advantage of a trade union dispute to bring discredit on the fair name of Belfast'.

In a note to Craig about the strike Dawson-Bates remarked that the rank and file (especially 'of our own kind') wanted to go back to work, feeling that they were caught in the Sinn Fein trap alluded to in the Orange Order's statement and wished to escape. But the Unionist leaders had to be cautious – they were certainly opposed to calling in the army, as was done in Glasgow that year.

The absence of the UULA from this conflict is striking, as is the fact that it was not sufficient for the Unionist leadership to demonstrate to trade unionists that the conflict was a Sinn Fein plot. The Grand Master of the Orange Order struck out of the manifesto a call for a return to work on the grounds that this was 'a little too arbitrary' and the document clearly and publicly backed the goals of the strike movement:

> Every Unionist candidate in the city of Belfast ... expressed himself in favour of better conditions and shorter hours for the workers, and we are asking them to keep that promise ... We have called upon our Unionist representatives in Parliament to at once insist on the claims of the workers all over the kingdom for a shorter working week ... We have received pledges from Edward Carson that they will do so.

The difference between the UULA and independent loyalism is that between night and day, and Sloan, Crawford and the Independent Orange Order represented an authentic working-class revolt within the heart of Unionism. In 1874 William Johnston of Ballykilbeg and his Protestant Working Men's Association controlled the local Conservative Party in much the same way as Archbold Salvidge and his Working Men's Conservative Association (WMCA) controlled the Tory party in Liverpool in the early years of the twentieth century.

The starting point was the same in both Liverpool and Belfast – the sheer weight of numbers of the working class which could not be ignored as the electorate steadily grew in size. John Charles Ryle, Anglican Bishop of Liverpool and a key figure in local politics, observed that without working-class support the Church of England in the city would have been in a minority position and Lord Derby flattered his audience at a WMCA meeting in Liverpool by telling them that they were numerous enough to put all the other classes into opposition. In the *National Review* article quoted above the author spoke of the working class as 'those who in truth control the Empire'. The nightmare would never cease: as political pressure slowly extended the size of the electorate, the ruling elite would more and more come to depend on 'the lower orders' to remain in power, and could never relax in its efforts to secure that support.

This dependence was even greater in Northern Ireland as, in the words of a UUC member, loyalist workers showed signs of a 'general desire to kick up against all authority and all discipline all over the Three Kingdoms'. George Hanna, an independent Unionist, was elected to represent East Antrim at Stormont, and Dawson-Bates feared that other independents ('people representing either labour interests or farmers' interests') would stand elsewhere in Ulster. Unionism could not exist without the loyalist working class, and the UULA, which gave no sign of rebellion or independence, appeared to be the ideal answer.

Southern nationalists considered these efforts to be a sinister plot, but in reality they were simply the expression of a different, but no less authentic, nationalism, which was the equal and opposite of the nationalism which developed in the South during the same period. In the crucial 1918 General Election de Valera succeeded in convincing Labour not to run candidates against Sinn Fein. The logic was exactly the same as that employed by Carson and Craig: anything which distracted the people of Northern Ireland from the struggle against Home Rule and independence was divisive and so potentially dangerous. A Unionist organisation had to be created to shelter Protestant workers from socialist temptation. Similarly, a Unionist Women's Association had to be set up so that, as Dawson-Bates put it, 'our women' did not become suffragettes.

The numerical weight of the industrial working class was much greater in Belfast than it was in Dublin, of course, so the pressure it created was that much stronger. Dawson-Bates, among others, was well aware

that the cross-class nature of Unionism could not
suppress all social tensions and that the co-existence of
all classes within Unionism hampered workers in
pursuing their specific demands. He fully appreciated
that this 'frequently leads to the younger members of the
working classes joining socialist and other extreme
organisations', and immediately after the First World
War therefore suggested the creation of working men's
clubs in Belfast 'to afford greater opportunity to the
working classes to belong to it [the UULA] and to prevent
them joining political Labour Associations whose
primary objects may be the advancement of Home Rule'.

That the Unionist leadership never entirely succeeded
in its attempt to channel all labour activity towards
Unionism is demonstrated by the protest movements of
the Protestant working class in 1907, 1911, 1919 and
1932, as well as during the Second World War. The
efforts made by the Unionist hierarchy to co-opt their
workers do provide a good indication of the loyalist
dream and of the way Unionists conceived the future of
their province. The Ireland dreamed of by nationalists –
rural, Gaelic-speaking and Catholic – is well known. The
corresponding Unionist dream was never as clear, but
the genuine pride shown by Carson and Craig when they
mingled with 'their' workers gives a valuable hint as to
what it contained, and we have already seen Craig
describing the election of the three working-class
Unionist MPs as the 'dream of his life'.

The Unionist dream was that of a prosperous
industrial province in which relations between bosses
and workers would be the continuation of relations
between benevolent masters and docile servants who
remained faithful to their masters even when times were
hard. In 1936 there was an attempt at establishing a
UULA branch in Londonderry and William Hungerford
wrote to S.F. Kennedy, a local employer, for information
about one Albert Nicholl, the prospective leader of the
new branch. Kennedy's reply was positive: Nicholl was a
respectable young man and a good worker. When a new

club was organised Kennedy confirmed the exemplary character of the other committee members: they were all 'willing workers without too much personal ambition'.

The UULA provides a fascinating insight into what, outside Ulster, are often considered to be the most unattractive features of the Protestant working class: religious sectarianism, moral conservatism and an obvious subservience to a system of political patronage. These emerge openly, sometimes almost as caricature, in UULA documents and speeches, but despite its occasional extremism the UULA's stance was not in fundamental disharmony with the mentality which prevailed more generally in the Unionist environment.

Positions like those adopted by the UULA are generally considered to be foreign to the labour movement, but a value judgement is necessary in order to eliminate all that is 'conservative' or 'reactionary' from working-class consciousness. Indeed, why should class consciousness not sometimes take a reactionary form? Male workers may decide that it is against their best interests that women should be employed in their industry, and they will be defending their 'collective class interest' should they object to the hiring of women. That opposition, like it or not, is just as much an expression of class consciousness as support for the dream of a socialist paradise. White workers may resist the employment of black workers on a New York building site or of Arabs in a Paris car factory, while Protestants may object to the employment of Catholics in Belfast's shipyards. This sort of prejudice will not disappear simply because socialists call 'class consciousness' that which conforms with their preconceptions and 'tribalism' that of which they disapprove.

There is of course the objection that class consciousness is by definition the awareness of more general interests, and that women, Jews, blacks and Catholics ought to be included in 'the working class'. But even here there is always a reservation: this inclusion takes place within national boundaries. Employees in North American and Western European companies try to defend their jobs and wages against competition from the low-wage, newly industrialising nations, and no one raises serious objections. In Northern Ireland Catholic and Protestant workers do not feel themselves to be citizens of the same country, so why should one group not protect its economic interests against the threat posed by the other community?

Belfast is an interesting city. It is strongly working-class, and the Unionist establishment's greatest fear has always been a direct confrontation with that working class. The reaction to the 1919 strikes was a classic example of that fear, as was the response to industrial unrest during the Second World War. But alongside their rebellious spirit Protestant workers have always displayed a massive attachment to the Union. This combination of rebelliousness and loyalism poses a question: has the Protestant working class sold out to the loyalist elite in return for protection under the Unionist umbrella? Has Unionism strengthened or weakened their hand?

While a great deal has been said about the alleged treachery of the Protestant working class, its power cannot be denied. It is difficult to imagine Southern workers organising the support of farmers, shop-keepers and others and successfully taking on all the major political parties, the media, the churches and the government to bring off a successful general strike, as the Ulster Workers' Council did in 1974. Although largely forgotten outside Northern Ireland, no one in Belfast has forgotten the lessons of 1974.

Paisley and Le Pen

It is obvious to anyone with a sense of Ulster's history that Ian Paisley models himself quite explicitly on Edward Carson, even going so far as to retrace the steps of the 'Carson Trail' and raise the flag of the Ulster Volunteers. But the heroic days of 1912 and 1921 are long gone: Carson was building a new state while Paisley has been trying to defend its ruins. Who today would unfurl a flag in a shipyard workshop, and in front of how many people? For all its anachronisms, however, Paisleyism is worth examining because, in the same way that many Catholics in West Belfast support Sinn Fein's outdated form of nationalism, so the DUP has become the representative of what is left of working-class loyalism.

When the National Front first burst onto the French political scene in the mid-1980s I began to listen to loyalist leaders in the light of that return of the far right to mainstream French politics and found a number of important similarities between the two political traditions. I even came to see certain physical resemblances between Jean-Marie Le Pen and Ian Paisley: the same thick-set figure, a similar stubborn forehead and authoritative chins. Both men also possess that particular eloquence which comes from open-air speaking.

I began to hear echoes of meetings in Paris and Marseilles when reading reports of rallies in Belfast:

> the crowd burst into a verse of 'Paisley is our leader' ... sung with the devotion and fervour of a people who really were prepared to follow the man who gave them leadership and guidance against a treacherous government.[6]

In the same way as Le Pen is a 'true Frenchman' born in Brittany, brought up to respect the virtues of *travail, patrie et famille*, so Paisley is a 'good Protestant', the descendant of those men who harnessed the power of running water, tilled the land and reclaimed the bogs. Before their arrival in Ulster plunder and misery ruled supreme, while after the plantation peace and prosperity prevailed. The boast of the family was that 'No Paisley ever married a Roman Catholic.' To this Ian Paisley added: 'From my head to my toes I am a Protestant, and if there is any dirt beneath my toenails, it is good Protestant dirt.'[7]

Ulster is the land of hard work, religious liberty and rock-solid faith which is being threatened by the

Catholic Church and the expansionist republican state. Given the deadly danger of that threat no language can be too strong when drawing attention to it. The Prime Minister of the neighbouring state, Charles Haughey, is nothing better than a gang leader:

> this guardian of murderers, this godfather of intended destruction, this green aggressor and fellow conspirator of Margaret Thatcher ... You will never ... get your thieving murderous hands on the Protestants of Northern Ireland because every drop of Ulster blood would be willing to be shed before we entered into your priest-ridden banana republic.[8]

The Roman Catholic church is not just any other church, it is the sworn enemy of all liberties, the 'harlot church, stained with the blood of the saints ... the servant of the antichrist',[9] while on a sunny day it might be described as the

> seed of the serpent ... Her clothes reek of the brimstone of the pit, her words and opinions label her the parrot of Beelzebub, her father ... We shall not be guiled. The dog will return to its vomit. The washed sow will return to its wallowing in the mire, but by God's Grace we will never return to Popery.[10]

But this is Paisley speaking, you may say – surely 'ordinary Protestants' don't mouth the same prejudices? Don't they? After all, most of them learned their political values not at school but in the streets, and 'No Pope Here', 'Not an Inch' and 'Remember 1690' are not so much phrases to be read in books as slogans painted on the gable-ends of houses in loyalist neighbourhoods.

Robert Harbinson remembers that as a boy he and his playmates calculated how much an ordinary Catholic would have to pay at confession for a week's sins. It was their firm belief that every sin had to be paid for in hard cash and that was why so many Catholics were publicans, their tills always full of money. The following lines were part of one of the first nursery lines that he learned:

> If I had a penny
> Do you know what I would do?
> I would buy a rope
> And hang the Pope
> And let King Billy through.[11]

Harbinson and his young friends feared and hated the Pope more than they feared Hitler, more even than they feared his loyal disciple over the border, Eamon de Valera. No wonder then that when Belfast was bombed during the Second World War and children were evacuated, the rumour spread among Harbinson and his young friends on the train that they were going to be taken across the border and would all be massacred. The children expected to see a frontier of 'battlemented walls, the moats and the vast palings with cruel iron spikes which must separate the dir⁺y Free State from clean and righteous Ulster'.[12] This vision of a border separating good from evil coincides with Ian Paisley's view of the difference between the North and the Republic, Protestants and Catholics. For Paisley Catholics are Catholics first, citizens of Northern Ireland second. They are required to disobey the law of the land if it clashes with that of Rome and are to all intents and purposes citizens of a foreign power whose values are hostile to 'our' fundamental principles.

These prejudices are taken up by leaders who are accomplished manipulators of doomsday emotions. They say loud and clear what traditional politicians are afraid to say: that the present is grim and the future will be even worse. They speak as men of the people, with the common sense of ordinary folk, whereas politicians and intellectuals are corrupt, timorous, faint-hearted and prone to compromise on what is sacred. When the Unionist leadership was first faced with the civil rights movement in the 1960s it thought that it could surrender certain of the Protestant community's privileges. Ordinary Protestants were worried. Who would pay the price of the promised reforms? Paisley gave them basic, simple reasons for resisting any change. The conflict was simply the continuation of the old war between Catholics and Protestants, and he never ceased to remind his followers that the Republic had not renounced its territorial claims on the North. For any social evil there is, depending on your point-of-view, always someone to blame: Le Pen will point the finger at Jews, Freemasons, Protestants and immigrants, Paisley at Catholics, lily-livered British politicians and compromisers in the Unionist camp. Those who do not share in this view are the fur-coat brigade isolated in their offices and comfortable in their large houses. In Belfast this liberal intelligentsia, concentrated in the south of the city, along the Malone and Lisburn Roads, no longer knows what the people think. Protected but weakened by their privileges, they no longer deserve to lead the country.

The appeal of such leaders can be traced to a clearly defined audience. When the times of change come those who are most afraid of that change are the most vulnerable, because in the past the only protection they had was the solidarity of a community which now faces destruction. With good reason they fear that they are going to have to pay the stiffest price for change. In other settings these people are often labelled 'poor whites' – small farmers, shop-keepers and unskilled labourers. The wealthy and the better trained are also the best equipped to face the new world, but those on the margins have nothing but long-established social networks to fall back on. If those crumble they will be left naked and unprotected, so they need to be reassured, and are naturally attracted by the reassertion of traditional values because those are their only strength. They know that they belong to a community whose main strength is quite simply its age and need to be told that they are superior for the simple reason that they were born in the right place (and possibly with the right skin colour). They share a common history, made up of myths, whether Joan of Arc or the Battle of the Boyne.

Carson spoke to a thriving Belfast while Paisley addresses a crumbling society. Change has disrupted long-standing solidarities without creating new ones. Industrial Belfast is now a shadow of its former self, but even though the shipyards are going and the old residential neighbourhoods are under threat of dispersal they continue to provide the basis of political imagery. There is therefore a growing feeling of instability and a desire for law and order as the threatened and insecure lend an ear to political leaders who tell them that the good old days were great and the present is threatening. In France many of those left out in the cold feel that with Jean-Marie Le Pen they have a new legitimacy in a world which ignores them. Le Pen's recurrent statements about the superiority of France and of Christian civilisation over that of the poorer nations echo loyalist speeches about the superiority of Ulster, the hard-working and prosperous Orange province.

These charismatic leaders passionately denounce any change, any attempt at reform and modernisation, as a betrayal of sacred beliefs. These tenets of the faith vary depending on local circumstances, and might be the surrender of Algeria if you live in Marseilles's la Canebière or the visit of the Pope if you live in Newtownards. The charismatic leader wages an uncompromising war, a crusade, against laxity and betrayal, the opening of pubs on Sunday or the building of mosques in Marseilles. They thrive on the prophecy of looming catastrophes that lack of faith is bound to cause and are adept at pointing to the scapegoat. The way in which Paisley describes Catholics and Le Pen points his finger at immigrants is disturbingly similar: both groups have large families, sponge on the dole, are slaves to their religion and are part of an international plot to destroy either Protestant liberties or Christian civilisation.

There is, however, a limit to the similarities. If the National Front is clearly rooted in the tradition of 'national populism' and of French fascism, the same cannot be said of Paisley and the trend he represents. When right-wing populism first appeared in France during the Dreyfus Affair in the 1880s it was faced with well established socialist organisations. Loyalty to a working-class community in France at that time was expressed through support for trade unions, co-operatives and political parties of the left. Right-wing populism could not compete with socialism on the same ground and so was obliged to adopt an extreme, xenophobic form. Protestant populism appeared in Northern Ireland in entirely different circumstances; as we have seen, it did not have to compete with a developed socialist movement because Northern Ireland's labour movement was confined to trade unionism and had no effective political voice. Protestant populism was therefore one of the channels through which class interests expressed themselves, and that is as true today of the DUP as it was of the Independent Orange Order in the late nineteenth century.

One of the most significant features of the French National Front is its sustained and violent attack on the welfare state. Le Pen's economic policies are firmly Thatcherite in their support for free enterprise and competition in every walk of life. Le Pen is also attracted to social Darwinism and nineteenth-century eugenics, believing that by helping the poor, the sick and the weak to survive the state enfeebles society as a whole by assisting the survival of its weakest and unfittest elements. These arguments would never be put forward by Paisley as the DUP is critical of the Republic of Ireland precisely because it abandons much of the responsibility for education and health, which Ulster Protestants consider to be the responsibility of society as a whole, to the private (religious) sector. As we saw when looking at the history of eighteenth-century Belfast, Ulster Presbyterianism was concerned to create the foundations of what we would now call a welfare state, and did so in a way which did not discriminate on grounds of religion.

What these two movements have in common is the logic

of exclusion. The community they dream of is culturally homogeneous, organised around fundamental values upon which there is no possible compromise. Those who do not share those values are to be excluded from the community and must be kept outside the walls. Be these 'others' Catholics in Northern Ireland or Moslems in France the logic is the same. They are a minority, but they represent a mortal threat because they are the advance party of a much larger population waiting to pour over the border.

To be a citizen of Ulster one must be a Protestant and to be a French citizen one must be a 'true-born Frenchman'. This logic is terrifying because it creates its an internal dynamic which, like a tumour, never stops growing. Whoever does not agree with Le Pen places himself outside the chosen few and becomes a 'bad Frenchman', and in the same way a Northern Ireland Protestant who resigns himself to compromise or reform becomes a traitor to Ulster. This, of course, is the logic of civil war. When the mechanics of inclusion and exclusion spread throughout the body politic in this way no one is spared. By way of response, the excluded, 'the others', tend to organise themselves into equally homogeneous and exclusive groups, as this is the only way they can grasp at the privileges or simple survival that is denied them by the dominant group. It is worthwhile pointing out, in this context, that the bombs and paramilitaries in Northern Ireland are the product of a logic of exclusion that is fully developed in the speeches of the French National Front. It is not by chance that Paisley and Le Pen express the same barely controlled violence and threat of the 'people's anger'. If you do not take us seriously, they say, you will soon have to deal with other, more sinister, men, shadowy figures against whom we represent the sole protection.

Notes

1 Philip Walker, *Democracy and Sectarianism, A Political and Social History of Liverpool, 1868–1939*, Liverpool 1981.

2 Miss Bates, 'So He Taught Them', *National Review*, November 1915.

3 John Gray, *City in Revolt*, Belfast 1985, p. 21.

4 Indeed, the nearest thing to an authentically fascist movement in Ireland was Eoin O'Duffy's fervently Catholic Army Comrades' Association, or Blueshirts, founded in 1931 in the South rather than any Protestant organisation in the North.

5 All the quotes about the UULA are drawn from its archives deposited in the Public Record Office, Northern Ireland (PRONI), files D 13227 and 1507. I would like to thank the staff of the PRONI for their aid in giving me access to those papers, and the Ulster Unionist Council for permission to use them. For a detailed study of the UULA, see my article in *Etudes Irlandaises*, December 1988.

6 Sam Wilson, *The Carson Trail*, Belfast n.d. (1982).

7 Ian Paisley, *These Twenty-Eight Years*, Belfast 1974, p. 10.

8 Ian Paisley, speech in Omagh, 13 February 1981, quoted in Wilson op. cit., p. 36.

9 Ian Paisley, *The Massacre of Saint Bartholomew*, Belfast 1972.

10 Ian Paisley, *No Pope Here*, Belfast 1982, pp. 81 and 88.

11 Robert Harbinson, *No Surrender*, Belfast 1987, p. 123.

12 Robert Harbinson, *Song of Erne*, Belfast 1987, p. 17.

7 Common Ground?

On the morning after the Enniskillen bomb I was having coffee at the Institute of Irish Studies of Queen's University. Not having a radio or a television in my flat I hadn't listened to the news and hadn't bought a newspaper that morning. Faces were tense and grim. 'What's happened?' I asked, breaking the terrible silence that hung over the room. Hadn't I heard? The day before eleven men, women and children had been killed in Enniskillen while remembering the dead of the two world wars. The IRA was bound to say that the bomb was a mistake, that it went off too early or too late, or that the warning had not got through, that the intended targets were 'only' soldiers and policemen not civilians ... Anyway, sorry. But the IRA scored a second, less newsworthy success: no one in this institute dedicated to the study of Ireland's past and present could even discuss this latest outrage.

The simple fact that the institute deals with Irish studies makes it suspicious in the eyes of certain sections of Belfast's loyalist population. Its Fellows are asked to stick to historical and academic subjects and to avoid current affairs because the institute has a constant fight to keep 'out of ' or 'above' politics. The policy is successful: the institute, like the rest of the university, appears to be a common ground where Catholics and Protestants can talk and study together. During the six months of my stay there I never heard on campus a single heated political discussion about any of the fundamental questions facing the North. Instead, there are meetings about apartheid, saving the rain forest and poverty in the Third World. History students can even invite David Irving, a British historian who believes that Hitler was more humane than you might think because he only really wanted to send the Jews to Madagascar and his subordinates organised the gas chambers and the ovens without his knowledge.

The meeting went off without any protest and I wrote a letter to *Fortnight* asking whether there was by any chance a connection between the fact that it is so easy in Belfast to kill someone on account of his or her religion and the lack of protest at the invitation extended to David Irving. The vice-president of the History Society took my question as an insult and replied with the old plea for 'freedom of speech'. But then didn't George Seawright use his freedom of speech to contemplate the final solution for Northern Ireland's Catholics?

There is a fundamental political debate taking place in Northern Ireland, and yet the province's major university seems to be a place where one can forget about this debate. Should a university really be a haven from the real world, a holiday camp, or should it be a place where this debate takes place in such a way that people's opinions will change and new food be provided for new thoughts?

As I observed earlier, something very strange happens when, as an outsider, you visit Belfast. Everybody appears to be liberal, tolerant and untainted by bigotry, so much so that you begin to wonder where the intolerance and the bigotry lie. Where do 'extreme' parties like Sinn Fein and the DUP get their votes? And the not-so-extreme, the SDLP and the OUP, which are nevertheless on opposite sides of the great sectarian divide, where do they get their votes from? And why do parties which try to work across the religious divide remain so marginalised and negligible in terms of a possible solution to the troubles?

'Common ground' is a misleading term. If by common ground one means a terrain on which both sides try to talk and engage in a dialogue so as to overcome their prejudices, then the common ground is very limited. The most frequently cited examples of the common ground, the universities, the trade unions and the minority of integrated schools are not places where this dialogue can take place because the essential precondition on which they bring together people from different denominations is to ask them to leave their religion, cultural background and guns at the door. Am I being unfair?

I have severe doubts about other pieces of so-called common ground: the Crown and other pubs in the city centre, the Lyric Theatre, certain sporting events, the Queen's Festival, the central shopping centre which is so quiet at night. In one sense I am unfair, I know, because it requires a very considerable effort for these places and events simply to exist, and they could all too easily crumble were it not for the dedication of a number of very hard-working people. It is, of course, vitally important that these places should exist as they provide an idea of what a peaceful Belfast might look like. Those people whose main efforts are devoted to keeping open these fragile areas where members of both religions can meet are right when they claim that the media are interested only in the most spectacular or photogenic aspects of the troubles and make very little of day-to-day examples of people working together across the sectarian divide. At the same time – and this is where my doubts creep in – the metaphorical guns are still in the cloakroom, and when leaving the Crown, Queen's University or the Linen Hall Library, people don't forget to pick up their guns any more than they leave behind their raincoats and umbrellas.

Whenever there is a conflict there are always places, generally for people with a better standard of living than the rest of the population, which provide a shelter from the thunder and lightning. These are places where it is considered bad manners to talk politics, to talk of the war, since they exist precisely to enable people to forget about the storm outside. I generally stay in Belfast for a

month, and people tell me that it is all very well for me to
deride these havens because after a few weeks of living
with the troubles I will be going back home to peaceful
Paris. But this objection does not drive away my
suspicions. During any war there are places of refuge
where people can avert their gaze from what is going on
around them and pretend that life is normal.

I spent six months in Belfast in 1988 pretending that
life was normal. I visited friends. I went to the Public
Record Office, guarded by wardens and high railings
which I no longer noticed after a while. I went to people's
homes for dinner. I went to the cinema or to see a play at
the Lyric. I drank in pubs and the next morning bought a
local paper to read the news of the previous night's
atrocities, which might have taken place anywhere in the
world but had that strange added thrill attached to any
piece of news which happens to take place around the
corner. I was able to walk to the place where the
explosion had taken place and feel the crunch of broken
glass beneath my shoes. It was the least I could do, I
thought, to give some credibility to the worries of my
friends back in Paris. The closest I came to Belfast's
everyday violence was when a bomb shattered my
kitchen window; had I been washing up at the sink, a
shard of glass could easily have sent me to the casualty
ward of the Royal Victoria Hospital.

There is not a single person in Belfast who has not
been touched by the violence in some way, who does not
have a relative, a friend or a colleague who has been
injured by a bomb, arrested for a while or intimidated by
the paramilitaries.[1] It is possible, of course, not to look
and so to pretend that these things do not happen and
that life in Belfast is like that in any other Western
European city. It is possible but, in the long run,
unsustainable. If a society is riven by intercommunal
violence in the way that Belfast is, then that violence has
to be looked into, analysed, discussed – and condemmed
and rejected.

After the Enniskillen bombing I was struck by the way

violence was part and parcel of the response of political forces on both sides of the religious divide. The loyalists cried out for more repression and called once again for the death penalty for IRA murderers. Sinn Fein and the IRA said the war would go on because the main reason for the violence was the presence of the British army. The SDLP claimed, somewhat inexplicably, that the bombing proved the validity of the Anglo-Irish Agreement. Nobody said, simply and straightforwardly, that the Northern Irish people did not deserve such atrocities. Violence was once again legitimised as it was the main 'proof' that everybody's policy was right.

The American author Sally Belfrage spent a year in Belfast in the mid-1980s writing a book which is as interesting for what it fails to see as for what it describes.[2] Describing Queen's University she writes of '8,000 students strolling around untroubled'. They're mostly Protestant, she adds rather dismissively, as if membership of that religion was a passport to an untroubled life. She is wrong on two counts: firstly because most of the students strolling on campus nowadays are Catholics, and secondly because they are not untroubled. If they really were so contented they would not want to leave so quickly to study or work on the mainland, in America or Australia, anywhere but Belfast. At the end of their studies most Queen's students move as far away from Belfast as possible. Why? Because they are untroubled? Sally Belfrage did not notice the troubles in Queen's because in such places they are, in effect, invisible. Just because bombs do not go off on campus this does not mean that the troubles are not present at Queen's; they are there in the spaces left by unspoken words.

The students' union is a non-sectarian body of which all students, Catholic and Protestant, are automatically members. The union, like the rest of the university, 'keeps out of politics', but its building is used almost exclusively by Catholic students. Slowly but surely Protestant students have stopped using its facilities,

even though student union officials will deny this. Why is
this the case? Could it be because there are Irish dancing
and Gaelic classes? No: students at Queen's are too
sophisticated to take offence at such relatively unimportant signs of cultural nationalism. The reason, more
fundamentally, is that this mixed body of students does
indeed mix in classes but, being mixed, the students do not
talk about the things that most vitally affect their lives.
They are cautious, and nobody wants to hurt anyone else's
feelings. It is only when you know who's who around you
that you talk freely, and talking freely is precisely what
relaxing is about. If you are in sitting in the students'
union common room after a lecture you want to chat and
have a joke, but in Belfast many jokes will, by definition,
be offensive to one section of the community. Maybe you
want to have a go at the British army and the mess it
caused when searching you aunt's house last night. Or, if
you're on the other side of the religious divide, you want to
moan about the so-called Anglo-Irish Agreement. You
can't relax in this way if you don't know who's who around
you or, more straightforwardly, if you know that there are
people from the other community sitting at the next table.

   This lack of dialogue and refusal to confront the major
problem facing society reminded me of a year I spent at
City College, New York, in 1975. City College is on 137th
Street in Harlem and, as in Queen's, the student body was
'mixed', which in New York, of course, doesn't mean
Protestant and Catholic but black and white, Jewish and
Gentile, English-speaking and Hispanic. Social life, however, took place around a racial divide. Just as the
students' union building at Queen's is to all intents and
purposes Catholic, so the social club at City College was
all black. In Belfast there is nothing as visible as the
colour of people's skin, so it is possible for Sally Belfrage
and others to pretend that Queen's is 'common ground'.
But is it?

Schools

As is well known, schools throughout Northern Ireland
are religiously segregated, and the uphill efforts to create
mixed schools on the model of the original Lagan College
deserve more than lip service. There can be little doubt
that people who have been to school with members of the
'other' community, be that Catholic or Protestant, black
or white, Jewish or Gentile, are less likely to grow up
holding prejudices against members of that community
than those who have been educated in segregated
schools. As someone from a country in which no religious
instruction is allowed in state-funded schools, I
wholeheartedly welcome the growing number of religiously mixed schools in Belfast. Such schools are, one
hopes, a small step towards an educational system which
will produce young people as free from religious bigotry
as is possible in a town like Belfast. At the same time,
however, I find myself wondering whether pupils in these
schools are allowed to discuss the issues which divide
them, or whether these cracks are papered over as they
are elsewhere in Belfast's 'common ground'.

Research into relations between Catholic and Protestant schools has uncovered a pattern of each side holding
a view of the other community's educational system that
says a lot about the double-bind in which Belfast's
would-be reformers find themselves.[3] As part of the effort
to 'build bridges' between the two communities there is
much official encouragement of visits of pupils and
teachers, sometimes parents as well, from Catholic to
Protestant schools and vice versa. The reaction of
Protestant visitors to the external trappings of the
Catholic religion was very revealing, because when they
saw pictures of the Pope, crucifixes and various other
pieces of religious paraphenalia in the school, many of
them were convinced that these had been put out
specially for their visit. They failed to appreciate that
this was how that particular school defined itself. The
reverse, of course, is also the case: the identity of

Protestant schools is expressed through pieces of loyalist iconography, and these were considered highly offensive by nationalist visitors. So what is to be done? If these external signs of cultural identity are removed, then on the next visit someone will say that all the tribal symbols have been removed specially for the occasion ...

The rules at government-funded Youth Training Centres, which cater for religiously-mixed groups of young unemployed, are clear. Political discussion is forbidden; flags and badges, any sign of politics, are also banned. Anything that reminds the trainees of the fundamental conflict, for which some people are willing to die or to kill, is simply forbidden. If I were running such a centre I am sure that I would enforce the same rules, because letting in badges and slogans is like letting in dynamite, and who wants explosives in a Youth Training Centre? The result, however, is that this religiously mixed group of young people co-exist as incomplete beings. Is this really common ground?

The Trade Unions

The trade union movement in Northern Ireland is often said to provide a common ground on which members of both religions can meet, work together for their mutual advantage and overcome their differences. Is this really the case?

The image of peace and unity between warring factions reconciled within the trade union movement was certainly very strong at the beginning of the current round of troubles. In August 1969 eleven people were killed and 800 Catholic homes burned down, but in the shipyards, the traditional starting point of previous anti-Catholic rioting, violence did not erupt on this occasion. Fifty shop stewards organised a meeting at which Sandy Scott, a trade unionist and member of the Northern Ireland Labour Party, denounced the violence which threatened the very existence of the shipyards. The meeting ended by adopting the following motion:

> This meeting of shipyard workers calls on the people of
> Northern Ireland for the immediate restoration of peace
> throughout the community. We recognise that the con-
> tinuation of the present civil disorder can only end in
> economic disaster. We appeal to all responsible people to
> join with us in giving a lead to break the cycle of mutual
> recrimination ... we demand that the government and the
> forces of law and order take stronger measures to maintain
> the peace.[4]

Congratulations poured in from the London and Dublin
governments and the major political parties supporting
the stand taken by Harland and Wolff workers. Sandy
Scott was rewarded with an MBE. Official bodies praised
the unions, and the following statement was issued by
the Northern Ireland Information Service:

> Sectarianism is contrary to trade union policy ... Members
> with all types of religious affiliation, as well as atheists and
> communists, have played a full part in the development of
> trade unionism ... With hardly an exception, sectarianism
> stops at the factory gate.

It is, to say the very least, unusual for a UK government
body to celebrate the active participation of atheists and
communists in trade unions, which just goes to show that
some words are more contentious and problematic than
others on Belfast's beleaguered 'common ground'.
'Atheists' and 'communists' are less controversial than
'Catholics' and 'Protestants', who are coyly referred to as
people of 'all types of religious affiliation'. In addition to
providing an intriguing insight into the psychology of
those who would like to encourage the growth of a
sanitised common ground, these two statements give a
clear picture of the policy of the trade union movement in
the North: maintain the peace and keep sectarianism the
other side of the factory gates – what happens there is
not the unions' problem and can be looked after by the
forces of law and order.

The earliest attempt at creating an all-Irish trades
union congress dates back to 1889. That first body was

short-lived, its fate sealed after it organised sporting events on a Sunday: Belfast trade unionists, scandalised by this failure to respect the sabbath, withdrew. Five years later, in 1894, the Irish Congress of Trades Unions was founded. The lesson of not causing offence to 'the other side' had been learned, and during the Home Rule crisis the congress could only survive by refusing to involve itself in the most controversial political issue of the day. Despite a further breakaway between 1945 and 1959, occasioned by the dispute about the Republic's neutrality during the Second World War, what is surprising is not the splits in the Irish trade union movement but the fact that Protestant and Catholic workers, despite their seemingly irreconcilable differences on the national question, are nevertheless members of the same organisation.

'Unity' is the dominant feature in the public image of the Irish Congress of Trade Unions and its Northern Ireland Committee (NIC). Elsewhere in Western Europe trade unions are labelled as left-wing or right-wing, skilled or unskilled, but in Northern Ireland they are first and foremost seen as havens of peace in a society at war. This image is seen by the unions as one of their main assets, and not surprisingly they and their allies do their best to project it as widely as possible. Dick Spring, the leader of the Labour Party in the Republic, reminded his audience at the New Ireland Forum that, 'The trade union movement has been many times a bulwark of responsibility in times of high political passion.'[5] Responsibility versus passion: we know who is going to win that particular argument, and the man who uses those words knows that he has already lost.

In any Belfast firm nowadays management will try to combat the obvious manifestations of sectarianism – flags and bunting are forbidden. In Shorts there was a clash between loyalist workers, who insisted on displaying the Union Jack, the flag for which their ancestors died, and the management. Everyone knew that what was removed was not really the symbol of the

British Empire but something much more local. So, out go the Union Jack and the tricolour, but does this banishing of the symbolism of sectarian struggle somehow mean that the underlying tensions are somehow spirited out of the factory?

When interviewed, a retired Catholic shipyard worker said that during all his time at Harland and Wolff he was never the victim of religious sectarianism in the yard, no one had ever bothered him about his religion or his political views.[6] What is extraordinary about this statement is that it is so obviously true: when loyalist workers weren't chasing Catholic labourers from the yard they simply left them alone. The result of this failure to talk about what is important is that the necessary words have gone rusty and the only language left is that of violence.

It would be difficult to imagine a more surreal situation than that which existed in Belfast in 1981 during the hunger strike. The city was in the grip of its gravest political crisis for a decade, but in its religiously mixed schools, its university and most workplaces there was silence. Words failed, and Belfast was the loser.

What, then, did trade unionists do during the hunger strikes? Quite simply, they battened down the hatches, kept a low profile and waited for the storm to blow over. For the Northern Ireland Committee of the Irish Congress of Trades Unions, the Belfast Trades Council and local union branches the hunger strikers were not political prisoners. Some of them were criminals, but at the same time the trade union movement knew that they were not 'ordinary' criminals. It was impossible to say nothing, but it would have spelt the end of the trade union movement had it supported the republican campaign in any way. The issue was fudged, and extraordinarily convoluted statements were issued stating that the prison system as a whole required reform and that conditions for all prisoners should be improved. No one was satisfied, but at least no one was so annoyed that the movement's unity was jeopardised.

Trade union leaders are always on the look-out to prevent 'politics' sneaking in through the back-door. What, one might think, could be more natural than for a union to take up the issue of discrimination in the workplace? In principle, the NIC supports the Fair Employment Agency, but has refused to take a practical stand on the question:

> The Committee's view is that, by and large, it should normally only intervene in issues arising from the reports at the request of the unions concerned or in the event of the NIC representatives on the Board of the Fair Employment Agency seeking assistance or guidance in the matter.[7]

The list of sensitive issues to be avoided is known by heart by all active trade unionists: paramilitary violence, discrimination, supergrasses, Diplock courts ... In almost any other city it would be easy for a union branch to condemn the absence of jury trial, but in Belfast it becomes a controversial issue as difficult to discuss in the trade union movement as in the students' common room at Queen's.

In summer 1986 the IRA decided that anyone entering army or police barracks for the purpose of trade, delivery or collection would be considered as 'legitimate targets' – there would be no distinction between soldiers or policemen and civilians who 'by their collaborationist actions release the same personnel for active duty'.[8] Doctors, priests and lawyers who have to visit barracks for professional reasons were advised to put distinctive stickers on their cars to avoid possible reprisals. Plumbers working at a police station or dustmen who empty the bins at an army post became legitimate targets, and in September 1986 a Protestant electrician was shot dead in his car, his 'capital crime' the alleged maintenance of military equipment.

An official of the Northern Ireland Public Services Alliance told me of the havoc, which he likened to shooting with a machine-gun in a crowded bar, that these tactics can cause. One of his members might work for twenty years in a politically neutral area of work and then be moved to a sensitive area. Overnight he becomes a 'collaborator' and so a 'legitimate target'. For a while panic spread and teams of people working together organised themselves into 'homogeneous' teams working in their own areas. There were a few strikes against intimidation, but nothing of any consequence. The campaign of union resistance to the IRA's threat to people going about their daily business petered out after a few months.

In the circumstances a unified trade union movement can only survive if one essential condition is met: local politics must not be discussed. Not a word can be said about the province's constitutional position or about any issue even remotely connected with sectarian conflict. The NIC, the trades council and union branches can condemn Conservative privatisation and industrial relations policies, can, like the students' union at Queen's, issue statements opposing apartheid, but not a word can be spoken about the hunger strikes. The pro-Communist French trade union, the CGT, led a vociferous campaign in support of the hunger strikers in 1981 and attended the Irish Congress of Trades Unions conference later that year; it has still to recover from its shock at the total silence on the issue at the conference.

The pressure of unemployment itself limits the influence of trade unionism as it pushes people out of the workplace and into their homes and communities. Young people go to school, the vast majority of them to schools segregated along religious lines. The small minority that goes to university will meet 'the other lot', and we have seen the artificial circumstances which surround that encounter. But for those who do not go on to further education the only other way of meeting members of the other religion would be in the workplace, but this possibility is greatly reduced by unemployment. So, after leaving their separate schools many young people find themselves unemployed and on the streets. Those who choose to involve themselves – laudably, one might think – in 'the community', in housing associations, cultural groups, youth clubs and so on, will inevitably be acting in a sectarian way because that work will benefit only members of their own religion. There is a fundamental difference between community organisations and trade unions in Belfast: the former cater almost exclusively for their 'own people', while the latter work for the good of members of both religions.

For all its shortcomings what is striking about the trade union movement in Belfast is the simple fact of its survival. It is an enormously strong nut which extremists on both sides have so far failed to crack.

Connolly Versus Walker

Sectarianism was built into Belfast's economic life and the religious colouring of the town's division of labour was a major influence on the development of its trade unionism. The organisation of unskilled labourers was perceived as a nationalist plot against the privileges of skilled Protestant men. For all their socialist and internationalist clothing, the most prominent syndicalist leaders, Larkin and Connolly, were to all intents and purposes nationalists. When Michael McKeown, one of Larkin's lieutenants, was trying to organise Belfast's dockers he arranged for Michael Davitt, a veteran of the Land League and one of the grand old men of Irish nationalism, to be on the platform at one of his meetings. The result was inevitable. The *Belfast Evening Telegraph*, apoplectic with rage, asked: 'Are the Orangemen of Belfast going to allow themselves to be led by a Fenian?'[9] The union split and the cross-channel dockers, the majority of whom were Protestants, left. Both Larkin and Connolly worked hard to organise Belfast's working people but, defeated because of their nationalism, moved South to greener pastures.

In the circumstances Belfast trade unionists who wanted independent labour representation had to be careful to remain 'non-political', which meant supporting the status quo, in other words favouring the Union and opposing Home Rule. In the South, on the other hand, trade unionists found themselves more and more involved in the struggle first for Home Rule and then for independence. Not alienating the bulk of trade unionists therefore meant adopting completely opposite positions in Belfast and Dublin. The issue was debated in the Irish Congress of Trades Unions. Northern delegates wished to retain the link with the British Labour Party, while Larkin and Connolly wanted to create an all-Irish Labour Party to form part of the all-Irish labour movement which they felt already existed.

In this debate Connolly represented Dublin and Walker Belfast. What followed was another episode of the 'dialogue' in different languages discussed in Chapter 1. Each side stated its opposing point of view and made no attempt to engage with or win over the other. Although Connolly would have hotly denied it, this showed that both sides had already accepted the logic of partition between North and South. Connolly never really gave serious consideration to Belfast politics while Walker remained firmly of the view that the city was the only place of any consequence in the entire island. Partition was a foregone conclusion. As a Labour candidate in Belfast, Walker constantly had to defend himself against accusations of being a supporter of nationalists and Home Rulers, and so described himself as a 'Labour Unionist' opposed to constitutional change. He believed that Protestantism meant dissent and that dissent could be equated with socialism. Connolly was therefore overjoyed at Walker's defeat at the polls in 1911. If elected Walker would have been the only 'Labour' MP to oppose Home Rule in the House of Commons; this, Connolly argued, would have killed any hope of socialism in Ireland for at least a generation. While this might have been true for Dublin, the reverse was the case in Belfast - had a socialist voted for Home Rule then the prospects for socialism in the North would be set back for half a century. As it was, the socialist flame was to be as thoroughly extinguished in Dublin as in Belfast in the decades that followed.

For Connolly there could be no socialism in Ireland without breaking the link with Britain. Walker did not claim to speak for Ireland but only for Belfast, and for him there could be no socialism in Belfast other than as part of the United Kingdom. Everything that had been achieved by way of improving the lot of the labouring classes in Belfast was possible because Northern workers were not isolated. The fight for democracy was more advanced in Britain than in Ireland, so Walker not unnaturally looked east across the Irish Sea rather than south to Dublin.

For more than half a century Connolly was seen as a revolutionary leader of world repute, the standard-bearer of easily recognisable values - nationalism, independence and a workers' republic - whereas Walker was enmeshed in a mean, narrow-minded and sectarian municipal socialism. Who would take Walker's side against Connolly? The problem is that in Dublin the majority did not take the path indicated by Connolly and Larkin, while in the North the majority of Protestant trade unionists recognised Walker's views as their own. In a democracy success and failure are generally assessed numerically: the majority wins and the minority loses, and Connolly must be recognised as the loser in his dispute with Walker. Connolly, who came to understand Dubliners quite well, did not really try to understand Belfast. No class in Ireland had the slightest interest in maintaining the Union with the United Kingdom, he claimed, even though it was quite clear that in Belfast the entire industrialist class and the greater part of the working class had every reason to support the Union and the link with the Empire. Their profits and their jobs depended on it.

The common ground in Belfast's trade union movement owes its existence to an artificial though pragmatic silence around the issues which divided Connolly and Walker.

Parties and Utopias

In the nineteenth century Belfast Catholics supported the Irish Parliamentary Party, and, after 1916, Sinn Fein; in the 1940s and 50s most Catholics voted for the (constitutionalist) Nationalist Party. Today the great majority votes for the SDLP or Sinn Fein. Most Protestants have always supported the Unionist parties, and still do, despite various efforts made by a Labour Representation Committee in the North. There is no equivalent in Northern Ireland of the British Labour Party, although there used to be a religiously mixed Northern Ireland Labour Party, which reached its highest level of support in 1962 when it held just seven of the 52 seats in Stormont. The British Labour Party was initially favourable to Home Rule and now, generally speaking, favours a united Ireland and so has no chance of attracting more than a handful of votes from the majority of Belfast's population.

The Campaign for Labour Representation nevertheless believes that the strong labour movement in Belfast and Northern Ireland should have a political party to represent it, just as it does in Britain. In other words, it wants the British Labour Party to stand candidates in Belfast and elsewhere in Northern Ireland. Not surprisingly, the campaign has been a failure, and part of the reason for this might be found in attitudes to the political levy. In Northern Ireland trade unionists have always had to opt *in* to the political levy, signing a declaration reading 'I hereby give notice that I am willing and agree to contribute to the political fund,' while in Britain trade unionists have to opt *out* of the levy. But what political party is to benefit from this levy? No one is really very interested. No money can be given to a political party in Northern Ireland as this involves support for a party with a particular view on the Northern Ireland constitution. The British Labour Party, as we have seen, has no electoral or institutional presence in Belfast. So in the case of London-based unions like the National Union of Public Employees the money goes to the British Labour Party, and to the Irish Labour Party in the case of Dublin-based unions like the Irish Transport and General Workers' Union. The unthinkable takes place: financial assistance flows from Belfast trade unions to a southern political party which accepts the Republic's constitutional claim to the North. When I mentioned this to a couple of loyalist trade unionists I thought they would be startled, but they did not even blink. I was talking to them of another world so alien and remote that it did not concern them. Labour parties, whether in Britain or the Republic of Ireland, are of minimal interest to the people of Belfast.

Both the Campaign for Equal Citizenship and that for Labour Representation argue that inhabitants of Northern Ireland are not the equals of those elsewhere in the United Kingdom. In London, Glasgow or Liverpool voters have an influence on the outcome of general elections, a say in putting a national party, Tory or Labour, in or out of power. In Northern Ireland voters are denied this basic right, and though the elections might be called 'general', they are in fact local elections and votes count only as expressions of support for or opposition to the link with Britain. The real choice is between nationalist parties (the SDLP or Sinn Fein) and Unionist parties (whether Official or Democratic). Since its foundation in August 1970 the Social Democratic and Labour Party has managed to retain support for constitutional nationalism throughout Northern Ireland, but, as is well known, faces stiff competition from Sinn Fein, especially in West Belfast and other parts of the city where the tribal war is most acute.

Non-sectarian political parties have made very little headway in Belfast. The Alliance Party was founded in April 1970, with Oliver Napier as its leader, to try to bridge the sectarian divide, but is now virtually irrelevant. Official Sinn Fein (from which Provisional Sinn Fein split in 1969) became Sinn Fein the Workers' Party and then, in 1982, simply the Workers' Party, but the more its changes of name reflected a move away from its roots, the more it has become alienated from its original supporters, Catholic nationalists, without making significant gains elsewhere.[10] There is, for better or worse, no room for non-sectarian political parties in Belfast.

Whichever way someone votes in Belfast, that vote will not really count in the overall context of the United Kingdom. As far as Westminster is concerned, votes cast in Belfast matter only for the purposes of deciding policy for Northern Ireland.

Suppose you live in Belfast and support the policy of the British Labour Party. You disagree strongly with Thatcherite economic policy, and you also happen to be fervently opposed to a reunified Ireland because you think that Belfast's future lies within the United Kingdom. You cannot vote Labour – after all, no Labour candidates stand anywhere in the North. You could vote for the SDLP, but then your vote would be counted as support for the Anglo-Irish Agreement and a united Ireland.

Or suppose that you are, in British terms, a Tory and that monetarist economic policies enjoy your whole-hearted support. More than that, you welcomed the Anglo-Irish Agreement when it was signed in 1985, and you still support it. If you vote for either Unionist party - Official or Democratic - your vote will be interpreted as a vote of opposition to the Hillsborough Agreement, and, as we have seen, a vote for the DUP is far from being a vote for Thatcherite economic policy.

To an outsider everything is very clear and logical. The answer to the problem is for the main political parties on the mainland to put up candidates in Northern Ireland, just as they do in any British constituency. Very simple. You only have to suppose ... The fundamental problem with this approach is that virtually nobody who lives in Belfast thinks along the imaginary lines outlined above. If the major British parties were to put up candidates in Belfast they would soon find out that their supposed electorate, if put to the test, would vote for the SDLP or Sinn Fein if Catholic and for the DUP or OUP if Protestant.

The Campaign for Equal Citizenship takes the province for a dreamland where the conflicts can be solved by waving the magic wand of mainland political parties. But the Labour Party has refused to contest elections in Northern Ireland and the mainland-type Conservative Party has not managed to take root in Belfast. There is no significant common ground in Belfast or elsewhere in Northern Ireland.

Notes

1 Trevor Barnes, *The Wounded City – Hope and Healing in Belfast*, London 1987, p. 11.
2 Sally Belfrage, *The Crack, A Belfast Year*, London 1987.
3 Dominic Murray, 'Schools and Conflict' in John Darby (ed.), *Northern Ireland, The Background to the Conflict*, Belfast 1983.
4 Quoted in Bill Rolston, 'The Limits of Trade Unionism' in Liam O'Dowd, Bill Rolston and Mike Tomlinson, *Northern Ireland: Between Civil Rights and Civil War*, London 1980.
5 Dick Spring, New Ireland Forum, *Report of Proceedings*, No. 1, 30 May 1983, Dublin 1983.
6 David Hammond, *Steelchest, Nail in the Boot and the Barking Dog, The Belfast Shipyard, A Story of the People Told by the People*, Belfast 1986, p. 40.
7 NIC statement, 1981.
8 IRA statement, 27 August 1986.
9 John Gray, *City in Revolt, James Larkin and the Belfast Dock Strike of 1907*, Belfast 1985, p. 25.
10 In 1990 the Workers' Party had just one representative on Belfast City Council; the contrast between this marginalised position and its status in Dublin, where the party's leader topped the poll in the 1989 European election, says a great deal about the changes taking place in the Republic and the deadlock in Belfast.

Conclusion

Belfast, as this book has been at pains to point out, has far more in common with other cities in Western Europe and North America than many people believe. It goes without saying, therefore, that the armed struggle which has dominated the headlines for the last two decades does not help us to understand Belfast any more than the troubles help in attracting new investment to the city.

When trying to decide which of its various plants to close and which to keep open, any sensible multinational company will almost inevitably choose to continue production at a more peaceful site than Belfast, so it is hardly surprising that many local people resent Belfast's 'bad image' and, looking around for a scapegoat, blame 'the media'. Throughout this book I have refrained from using the phrase 'bad image' because to do so would imply that Belfast is really a peaceful city where every now and then an untoward sectarian murder or a fatal police blunder disturbs the peace, even though these incidents are on the whole less frequent in Belfast than in many American cities. Because of the media, apparently, every blast is over-represented in the news and outsiders think that Belfast is as dangerous as Beirut. The argument goes that, if only someone were able to cajole journalists into taking a stroll in the Botanic Gardens in the spring and enjoying the delights of the Belfast Festival in the autumn before writing their stories about the city, money would pour into Belfast and the hotels and bed-and-breakfasts would be jammed with delighted tourists and feverish businessmen.

The difficulty with the 'bad image' theory is not that Belfast's image is bad but that Belfast's problem is not just one of image. For all that photographers working in Belfast might occasionally set up a dramatic shot, sectarian strife and political instability are not created by journalists baying for blood and a good story, and it has to be said that the foreign and, to a lesser extent, the British media have become tired of a seemingly endless and repetitive story. How on earth can the Northern Ireland Tourist Board claim that tourism could become one of the major industries in the North if only the province's 'bad image' could be overcome? If young people leave Belfast at the first possible opportunity is this because of the city's bad image or because of their own experience of living in the city? The largest headlines after an explosion are to be found in the province's own papers, which only proves that what really concerns people is the fate of their city, and that fate is intimately linked with the armed conflict.

It is nevertheless true that Belfast's image can often be irritating for anyone who lives there, even briefly. When I told friends in Paris that I was going to live in Belfast for six months some thought that I must be brave or foolhardly, and came out with the standard jokes about bullet-proof jackets and tin helmets. Others voiced genuine worries: 'Isn't it dangerous? Aren't you afraid?' I tried to explain that in 1986 more people had been killed by terrorist bombs in Paris than in Belfast, that I would be just as safe in this Irish Beirut as in my home town, but all to no avail – my friends continued to think of Belfast as a city at war.

Why French people – and no doubt many other foreigners – consider that they live in a 'normal', peaceful society while Northern Ireland appears to them to be torn apart by sectarian feuds often puzzles me. *La belle France* has its fair share of sectarian murders and paramilitary activities, and hardly a week goes by without an Arab or an African being beaten to death by racist gangs. 1990 even saw a return to the worst form of

anti-semitic outrage with the disinterring of a recently
buried corpse in a Jewish cemetery near Le Pen's
stronghold in Marseilles. Yet nobody would dream of
saying that France is a country at war or accept the need
for emergency legislation. So what is it that distinguishes
Marseilles from Belfast?

The difference, at the end of the day, is that Belfast
really is at war. War is not defined by the number of
bombs and casualties but as a state of mind and the
acceptance as a fact of life of Clausewitz's dictum about
war being the pursuance of political ends by other means.
It is very obvious that in Belfast there is a war in people's
minds, even if it is not always on their doorsteps.
Everyone in the city knows that any move by a
paramilitary group is just as important as an election
manifesto, inter-party agreement or a strike, and often
more so.

War is the great simplifier. A barricade has only two
sides, and there is no common ground at either end of
this scar which divides a street or a society. War excludes
anything not related to the supreme aim of victory, which
explains why to the outsider Northern Ireland seems to
be an oasis of certainties in a world of doubt.

In most Western countries the current crisis· is not
confined to unemployment and housing conditions,
however dreadful these may be, but extends to people's
perception of the society in which they live. Politics used
to be primarily about the opposition between capitalism
and socialism, and in those far-off days the answers often
outnumbered the questions. In France the Socialists
came to power in 1981 and, although they at first tried to
strike out in a new direction, the changes were not dramatic and disillusion soon became widespread. Politicians,
however, have to sound confident and their speeches still
overflow with certainties, but ordinary people continue to
have important questions which they feel are
unanswered. There seems to be no easy way out of the
universal problems of unemployment, urban insecurity,
ecological catastrophe and terrorism ... the list is endless.

In France only Le Pen's National Front has an instant solution: there are 4 million unemployed and 4 million immigrants – send home the immigrants and every 'true-born Frenchman' will have a job. It is scarcely surprising that such simplistic ideas should be linked to a militaristic view of politics.

Belfast is still a place of certainties. Unemployment and the crisis of the economy are obviously closely inter-related with the troubles. For some people a reunified Ireland will provide investment and jobs, while for others the main reason for the city's economic decline is the presence of a rebellious and unruly minority. Reunify the island or tame the minority, depending on your tribal affiliation, and Belfast will flourish once more. Are these 'solutions' any more useful or realistic than Le Pen's answer to France's ills?

In 1987 I saw Stewart Parker's *Pentecost* at Belfast's Lyric Theatre, and the play only served to underline this point. The characters on the stage were perfectly 'normal' by current Western European standards: a wife who had been beaten up by her husband, an unemployed musician, a woman in the middle of a divorce and a young man trying to find himself and somewhere he might belong. Remove the background of the troubles and you might have the same characters facing the same problems in Liverpool, Marseilles or Milan. But the war cannot be suppressed or written out – it is not simply a stage-setting that can be changed at will, but an all-pervading reality. The play's message seemed to be that the troubles were at the root of the characters' problems and dilemmas: re-establish peace and everyone would be happy. If only it were that easy.

In the winter of 1942 in France a child was sitting alone in a bus, listening to a group of adults complaining about the hardships of life. Food was scarce and expensive, schools were far from their homes, there was no coal to heat the house. One of the women then said, 'And on top of that we have this war.' 'On top of that' – the child could not believe his ears. What on earth could she mean? The child came from a middle-class family, and for him the scarcity of food, cold houses and long journeys to school through the snow were exactly what war meant. Could it be that some people lived like this all the time, and that for them war was yet another burden?

Maybe the people of Belfast will discover what that French child found out in 1942. When they say, 'On top of that we have the troubles,' then the nightmare will really begin, but at least, if this is a comfort, they will share it with us all.

Index